PRAISE FOR
WHAT WE TALK ABOUT
WHEN WE TALK ABOUT BOOKS

"Leah Price's radiantly intelligent book makes us rethink and re-view the endlessly alive, endlessly shape-shifting and self-reinventing activity that is reading. Its cracking readability—when was the last time you had to disable the Wifi for a book on books?—should not disguise how cogently and coherently it is argued, and the depth of learning with which its arguments are meticulously substantiated. It is also profoundly witty, funny, and beautifully written. (When was the last time you thought that about a book on books?) You emerge, after turning the last page, a smarter, better informed, joyous person."

—NEEL MUKHERJEE, Man Booker Prize finalist
and author of *The Lives of Others* and *A State of Freedom*

"At once authoritative and accessible, Price's account busts many myths about both the past and the future of reading. Long may it keep us talking about books!"

—WILLIAM H. SHERMAN, director,
Warburg Institute, University of London

"Predictions of the death of the book weren't only greatly exaggerated; as Leah Price notes in *What We Talk About When We Talk About Books*, they were old news. The book has survived numerous death sentences in the past, and this time, as before, it's been the occasion to reinvent old practices of reading. What the Victorians called 'furniture books' continue to adorn coffee tables and the Ikea shelves widened to accommodate them. People still hold books in their laps on couches and in coaches (enjoying the 'library atmosphere' of Amtrak quiet cars). Self-help books have their roots in the 'bibliotherapy' proposed a century ago. It is still a very book-ish world that we inhabit, and I know of no guide to it wittier and more engaging than Leah Price, whose insights, erudition, and aperçus had me dog-earing every other page."

—GEOFF NUNBERG, resident linguist, NPR's *Fresh Air*

WHAT WE
TALK ABOUT
WHEN WE
TALK ABOUT
BOOKS

ALSO BY LEAH PRICE

How to Do Things with Books in Victorian Britain

Unpacking My Library: Writers and Their Books

The Anthology and the Rise of the Novel:
From Richardson to George Eliot

WHAT WE TALK ABOUT WHEN WE TALK ABOUT BOOKS

The History and Future of Reading

LEAH PRICE

BASIC BOOKS
New York

Basic Books
Hachette Book Group
1290 Avenue of the Americas, New York, NY 10104
www.basicbooks.com

Printed in the United States of America

First Edition: August 2019

Published by Basic Books, an imprint of Perseus Books, LLC, a subsidiary of Hachette Book Group, Inc. The Basic Books name and logo is a trademark of the Hachette Book Group.

The Hachette Speakers Bureau provides a wide range of authors for speaking events. To find out more, go to www.hachettespeakersbureau.com or call (866) 376-6591.

The publisher is not responsible for websites (or their content) that are not owned by the publisher.

Print book interior design by Jeff Williams.

The Library of Congress has cataloged the hardcover edition as follows:

Names: Price, Leah, author.
Title: What we talk about when we talk about books : the history and future
    of reading / Leah Price.
Description: First edition. | New York : Basic Books, 2019. | Includes
    bibliographical references and index.
Identifiers: LCCN 2019004657 (print) | LCCN 2019019847 (ebook) | ISBN
    9781541673908 (ebook) | ISBN 9780465042685 (hardcover)
Subjects: LCSH: Books and reading. | Books and reading—History. | Books and
    reading—Technoligical innovations. | Books—History. | Literature and society.
Classification: LCC Z1003 (ebook) | LCC Z1003 .P9 2019 (print) | DDC 028—dc23
LC record available at https://lccn.loc.gov/2019004657

ISBNs: 978-0-465-04268-5 (hardcover), 978-1-5416-7390-8 (ebook)

LSC-C

10 9 8 7 6 5 4 3 2 1

CONTENTS

INTRODUCTION

W HEN THE FIRST Waldenbooks opened in my hometown in the 1970s, its self-help bestsellers urged my
parents to schedule date nights. A quarter century later, my
generation, too, began to feel guilty about letting chores crowd
out deep relationships. But what we lusted for wasn't a person.
Our fantasy was to reconnect with books.

That love felt star-crossed. One Sunday morning in 1992, the
New York Times sprawled across my doormat predicted "The
End of Books." Could print, asked the novelist Robert Coover,
survive the age of "video transmissions, cellular phones, fax
machines, computer networks"? Coover wondered, but other
essayists judged. In 1994, the window display of an independent
bookshop that would be evicted a few months later to make
way for a Starbucks led me to a hardcover called *The Gutenberg
Elegies*. In its pages, ex-bookseller Sven Birkerts mourned the
"focused, sequential, text-centered engagement" that he worried was being jostled aside by "the restless, grazing behavior of
clicking and scrolling."[1]

Soon, newfangled blogs had me mousing through to surveys proving that even if book-length works continued to be read, it wouldn't be by men, or in the bathtub, or off the beach. In 2004, the National Endowment for the Arts released a survey of American reading habits—or rather, the lack thereof. The resulting report, *Reading at Risk*, identified a 14 percent decline in literary reading since 1992, with rates especially low for men and young adults. In 2007, a follow-up report appeared under the title *To Read or Not to Read*. The practice of engaging with texts, the riff on Hamlet suggested, was at existential risk. Once again Americans seemed to be reading less and reading less well, with 19 percent of seventeen-year-olds reporting that they "never or hardly ever" read. Meanwhile, 28 percent of teenagers who *did* read reported combining the activity with the simultaneous use of other media.[2]

As magazines migrated from doormats to laptops, articles vied to diagnose the disappearance of a way of life that Americans had once read. Just as often as the death of print journalism, though, journalists lamented the decline of printed books. When Nicholas Carr asked in a 2008 *Atlantic* article "Is Google Making Us Stupid?," the evidence for answering in the affirmative was the fate of long-form reading. "Immersing myself in a book or a lengthy article used to be easy," Carr confessed, but in the digital era he found himself "getting fidgety," "dragging my wayward brain back to the text."[3] What was lost wasn't just the information that he was no longer absorbing, but the taste for being absorbed.

My first smartphone strafed my pocket with predictions that even if reading survived, eyes would glaze over before the 141st character. Essays of every conceivable length braced us to mourn the habits of mind or even soul that books had once occasioned: the capacity to follow a demanding idea from start to finish, to look beyond the day's news, to be alone. As our shelves emptied out, we feared losing our selves.

———

Here's what happened instead. Sales of printed books rebounded in the decade that followed—rising as steadily as electronic book sales leveled off.[4] In the United States, 2011 was the first year in which more ebooks were sold than hardcovers; by 2016, though, hardbacks were outstripping ebooks once again.[5] And since most of the books we read weren't bought yesterday, it may be even more telling that in that same year, twice as many Americans read glued or sewn wood pulp than read an electronic book.[6] As I upload this manuscript late in 2018, new industry reports inform me that print sales have increased in the United States for each of the past four years.[7] Last year, sales revenue from hardbacks and paperbacks outstripped revenue from ebooks by more than $300 million.[8] Also late in 2018, the Association of American Publishers reported revenue from hardcover sales up around 3.5 percent, with revenue from digital books down nearly as much.[9] And in December 2018 as well, gift-givers found best-selling titles ranging from a Richard Powers novel to a Frederick Douglass biography on back order. One culprit turned out to be that most old-fashioned of crises: a paper shortage.[10]

It's true that bookstore sales and revenues have declined in the past decade. But the fact that the dip began right after the 2008 recession suggests that the culprit is financial, not technological.[11] And it's true that a third of Americans in their late teens and twenties reported reading an ebook in 2017, twice the rate of their counterparts over sixty-five.[12] But the youngest Americans believe, at least, that printed books won't die off when their grandparents do. While in 2012, 60 percent of six- to seventeen-year-olds surveyed had predicted they would always prefer print to ebooks, by 2016, that number had climbed a modest but significant 5 percent.[13] Old media isn't just the province of the old.

More fundamentally, the pages that follow will try to persuade you that the digital-age printed book isn't really an old medium at all. Rather, it's a format being reinvented by booklovers before our eyes. In that sense, our own era continues, rather than breaks with, a tradition of innovation that has seen new formats emerge over and over again for half a millennium.

Like book owning, book borrowing doesn't just appeal to my middle-aged peers. In 2016, the Pew Trust found that adults under thirty-five were likelier than their elders to use a library.[14] One explanation is that parents of young children remain the most frequent visitors, but another is that libraries themselves were changing. Long providers of tax advice and public bathrooms, imaginative librarians now lent out interview suits and fondue sets.[15] As journalist Susan Orlean points out, libraries found themselves stretched in ever more directions to provide "voter registration and literacy programs and story times and speaker series and homeless outreach and business services and computer access and movie rentals and ebook loans and a nice gift shop. Also, books."[16] Librarians lobbied for public access to research findings; they taught patrons to assess the legitimacy of new sources; they offered floor space to patrons unhoused by hurricanes.[17]

Meanwhile, outside of the buildings officially designated for buying or borrowing them, books began to be handed out by volunteers on subway platforms, donated to barbershops in neighborhoods devoid of bookstores, and read aloud (in programs called Paws to Read or Tails of Joy) in order to calm cats and dogs cooped up in shelters. No longer just a tool to ferry information from one brain to another, reading began to look like a panacea.

Fear seemed to have goaded booklovers into action. And alongside the urge to rescue reading came the itch to understand it. College courses on media history mushroomed. National health institutes funded randomized trials to test whether reading raises serotonin levels, lowers body-mass indexes, or combats insomnia and Alzheimer's.[18]

As scientific journals migrated online, the articles in them variously compared print reading with screen reading, book reading with magazine reading, fiction reading with nonfiction reading, literature reading with the reading of whatever genres they identified as antonyms to the literary. Some credited the curative power of reading to its content (books whose characters ate healthfully seemed to curb their readers' snacking), but others focused instead on its medium (print vs. online), its scale (immersive prose vs. snippeted listicles), or its life expectancy (durable books as opposed to ephemeral articles).

Thus reading garnered testimonials from an unlikely quarter: science.[19] Or more precisely, *Science*. In 2013, that journal published a study concluding that reading about fictional characters correlates with more sophisticated theory of mind. More specifically, reading about characters in formally ambitious "literary" fiction did—for the authors discovered experimental subjects to be better at identifying the emotions expressed on faces or at understanding others' false beliefs when they had just read prizewinning short stories than when they had just read less esthetically ambitious popular fiction.[20] This latest version of the centuries-old attempt to distinguish trashy escapism from intellectually challenging and therefore morally respectable fiction was widely reported by journalists with their own investment in reading.

Neuroscientists drilled down, wedging readers inside fMRI scanners to measure novels' effects on "brain function and structure."[21] Social scientists scaled up: psychologist Steven Pinker's 2011 book *The Better Angels of Our Nature* correlated a centuries-long decline in violence with an increase in fiction reading. Some studies measured effects on health; others on wealth; yet others on civic virtue. Back in 2004, data aggregated by the National Endowment for the Humanities suggested that Americans who read outside of work and school were likeliest to vote and volunteer. Four years later, a meta-analysis connected the frequency with which Canadians read books to the rate at which they donated and helped their neighbors.[22] Also in 2008, a British study correlated pleasure reading inversely with divorce.[23] Madame Bovary would have been surprised.

As a literature lover, I, too, clutched at the kind of self once forged—unpredictably, unreliably, but also unstoppably—in encounters with a page. Switching my phone back on every time I exited a climate-controlled reading room, I chafed at the alerts and tweets from which Special Collections had briefly cocooned me. (Then again, I felt the same way on exiting jury duty.)

As a scholar, though, I began to wonder whether the past against whose glories I measured my frazzled present were a figment of my imagination. I'm not just a literature lover, but also an English professor. When I entered graduate school at the end of the last century, my life was changed by learning from librarians how to look at books as objects—as hunks of paper, ink, and glue whose look and feel and smell hold clues about the now-dead hands through which they passed before reaching mine. And over the course of the two decades that I've spent teaching Harvard undergraduates the field known as book history, I became less and less sure that books had ever commanded anyone's undivided attention.

Poetry collections whose crisp corners hinted that they'd never escaped the coffee table; romance novels crumpled from being hidden in an embarrassed teenager's pocket, with well-fingered pages of seduction scenes interrupting landscape description whose pages retained like-new crispness; political polemics stained with beer from being read aloud at the pub to listeners too poor to buy their own copy, too illiterate to read to themselves, or too encumbered with a card game to hold their own book—each genre testified that serious, silent, solitary cover-to-cover reading has never been more than one of many uses to which print had been put.

It's true enough that print experienced a golden age between the rise of mass audiences in the eighteenth century to the Cold War–era triumph of the paperback, by way of public school systems, cheap wood-pulp paper, browsable bookstores, and taxpayer-funded libraries. Parts of this story, though, began to strike me as unhelpful or even untrue. One is what I'll call the myth of exceptionalism—that is, twenty-first-century readers' sense of living through an unprecedented change. The more I tried to figure out how much time different societies had actually carved out for reading, the more the data confirmed that successive audiovisual media did indeed chip away at the dead time once filled by books. I was surprised, though, to find that the strongest proof of print's vulnerability to competition wasn't the smartphone. The best-documented such competitor turned out to be TV, whose arrival in the Netherlands in the 1950s, for instance, coincided with a dramatic and elegantly charted drop in rates of pleasure reading.[24] The problem, I began to think, didn't lie in our devices so much as in our schedules. When we mourn the book, we're really mourning the death of those in-between moments (waiting in line, riding a bus) that nineteenth-century changes in lighting and transportation made hospitable to light reading, and that twenty-first-century communications infrastructures made available to paid labor.

Equally unhelpful is the myth of the ideal reader. Whether they blame our vices on the failure to read or blame the failure to read on our vices, digital-age defenders of print equate reading with virtue. Unfortunately for this hypothesis, the golden age of print was hardly a golden age for the habits of mind that digital natives trust the book to induce. Print, Chapter 2 will try to persuade you, has inspired efficient multitasking more often than rapt attention. And while some readers may have lost themselves in a book until their surroundings faded around them and they forgot all sense of time, we'll see in Chapter 3 how consistently bedtime stories have paced circadian rhythms and morning papers have numbed commutes. The printed books now being deployed to cure mental and physical ills spent much of their long life, as Chapter 4 details, under suspicion of sickening and maddening their readers.

Finally, the myth of the self-made reader—of an unmediated communion between a reader's mind and an author's—erases all the third parties who sell books, lend books, catalog books, give or withhold them. Searching for alternatives to this individualist account of reading, I found my way to the activists whom we'll encounter in the final chapter. Unlike essayists who champion reading as training for solitary self-sufficiency, these community organizers treat books—whether printed or electronic—as a means to connect the human beings who exchange them.

Each of these myths credits long-form print with producing a certain kind of individual. A longer view, though, makes books' effects look less predictable, beginning with the simple question of whether they get read at all. Well before competition from social media, only a tiny minority of the volumes that rolled off the presses ever found a reader—let alone sparked the focus that smartphone-fingering fidgeters dream of recapturing. Instead of plodding from page 1 to The End, the early readers whose traces I hunted down in libraries turned out to have hopscotched around chapters. Instead of giving novels their undivided attention, aristocrats had their hair curled while listening to a servant read aloud. Instead of respecting the anthology's boundaries, poetry lovers scissored pages apart to paste scraps of one collection into the margins of another.

In short, printed books gave birth to many of the capacities—and dangers—for which digital devices are now being faulted. Long before playlists, amateurs reshuffled and recombined snippets into new collections. Long before anyone spoke of "spreadable media," texts survived in epigraphs for other texts. Long before anyone fretted about Amazon displacing bookstores, bookshops sold fish while clothing peddlers backpacked pamphlets door to door. Authors debated in print, as strenuously as today's content providers do online, whether the written word should be rented or sold, licensed or owned, linked in or locked down.

What's driving digital-age debates about print, I began to realize, may be as much a mood as a belief. That mood is fear. We may be seeking refuge from technological and commercial upheavals, from the people and places that crowd in on us, or from our own sickness and weakness. The problem is that treating the book as a bunker may shortchange its potential to engage with the world—not just with the world represented by its words, but with the world of other human beings who made or transmitted the object itself. Yes, the book can be a shell (essayist Alberto Manguel reminisces that "my library was my tortoise shell") but it can also be an antenna or a spear.[25] Seeing books thrust into the service of comfort and sanity and good taste, I started wanting to recover the book's power to upset and unsettle and even anger readers.

Digital-age essayists can idealize books only by dint of imagining that reading has always meant curling up alone with a novel purchased for hard cash, read cover to paperback cover. The book historians whom we'll meet in the next chapter, though, insist that the characteristics we associate with reading now haven't been around forever, let alone been bundled into a single package. In ancient Rome, texts circulated as papyrus scrolls; even after early Christians adopted the gathered pieces of paper called the codex, their raw material was animal skin, not paper. The movable type invented in the fifteenth century didn't enable mass production until the substitution of wood pulp for old clothes drove down papermaking costs four hundred years later. It's even more recently that retail sales nudged out books printed at the author's expense, bankrolled in advance by subscribers whose names appeared at the front of the book, or subsidized by a dedicatee. Ebooks form only the latest of these many chapters.

Nor is competition among media anything new, for even at its height, print never clawed out more than a niche in a crowded landscape. Right up to 1789, the most influential political newspapers in Europe were hand-copied by professional scribes. As a more flexible, more discreet, more distributed technology than print, handwriting allowed radical writers and publishers to both avoid censors and create a loyal coterie audience that forged collective identities through the act of forwarding or exchanging materials.

Those activities may sound uncannily like blogging or tweeting. In fact, a missing link connects the handmade with the digital. The oldest distribution technology (hand copying) and the newest (the internet) flank mid-twentieth-century media like the mimeograph, the hectograph, and the microfilm, now too old to be sexy but too new to be quaint.[26] During the Cold War, in the Eastern bloc and parts of Southern Africa, photocopiers shaped the circulation of news, providing a middle ground between handwritten documents (nimble, private, and participatory, good at cementing communities of like-minded individuals but inefficient for reaching large anonymous audiences) and the printing press (high start-up capital but low running costs, facilitating standardization but discouraging interaction, easy to scale up but also to regulate).

From its beginnings, as each of these episodes suggests, print changed in step with the media that surrounded it. And even at any given historical moment, printed books took different forms and prompted different behaviors. Only by ignoring both kinds of variation can we make a monolithic printed past into a stick with which to beat our digital present. The more long-dead readers I encountered on the pages of the books that they'd once borrowed or owned or read or handled, the more differences within the world of printed books seemed to outstrip differences between print and digital.

The more reading changed before my eyes, the more precedents I recognized in earlier moments of media history that had seemed just as dramatic in their own time. The more I studied book history, in contrast, the harder-pressed I was to find any precedent for the content of digital-age beliefs *about* print. For while debates about its effects were very old, the emotional tone of those debates had shifted, within not much more than a generation, from fear to hope.

Throughout the first few centuries of its existence, experts had already assumed print to be life changing—but with the exception of a few sacred texts, that change was most often thought to be one for the worse. Ministers warned against the distractibility engendered by squandering time and eyesight over a novel. Doctors diagnosed newspaper addicts, sickened not just by the ideas transmitted but by the sheer experience of wallowing in a wood-pulp world. The literate classes themselves felt embarrassed about what they read, or meant to read, or wished they hadn't wasted a night devouring.

In fact, once the mechanization of papermaking and the spread of state-supported schools led to near-universal literacy in the West a few centuries after Gutenberg, reading provoked new anxieties. Best-selling lists of what to read were joined by bestsellers advising on how to read, and how not to. Trawling through these early how-to books, the French historian Roger Chartier realized that as the mere fact of being able to read came to be taken for granted, and as new technologies and changing laws multiplied the number of books owned by the average household, the distinction between literate and illiterate people gave way to finer distinctions within the reading public. To read was no longer enough. Nor was the trick even to read the right books. Rather, you now had to read in the right place, at the right pace, at the right time of day.

Then, as now, policy makers debated demographics: who's expected, required, or forbidden to read. They debated economics: Should print be sold or rented, lent or gifted, repaired or trashed? They argued even more vehemently about what would eventually come to be called ergonomics: the proper positioning of the hands that held books and the laps on which they lay. The history of reading is also a history of worrying, and those worries rule out any clean contrast between bookish virtue and digital vice.

Only toward the end of the last century, as these anxieties about the guilty pleasures brokered by print gave way to diatribes against the addictiveness of ubiquitous, always-on electronic information, did books change from the problem to the solution. Where gentlemen had once fretted about the shilling shockers devoured by their wives, children, or servants, now bloggers began to confess, with rueful self-mockery, to their own inability to finish a book. And just as the printed codex caught on only once it became cheap and portable enough to be consumed with an efficiently divided attention (read aloud at the hairdresser's in the eighteenth century, skimmed on a Victorian train), so too did past anxieties about paper anticipate present concerns about screens.

Hand-copied, recited, gifted, exchanged, printed books were the first social media.[27] They started conversations; they started fights; and they connected each reader to others. The American and British librarians, booksellers, and activists to whom this book gives the last word are once again enlisting printed books to forge community. Instead of defending the page from the screen, though, they repurpose digital tools to circulate printed books. Proofreading and uploading classic texts, logging the location of book giveaways, posting smartphone snapshots of their bedside book piles, using social media to publicize collective reading aloud, these booklovers don't confine their efforts to texts that happen to be about community. Rather, their ambition is to bind readers together by the act of distributing books, or even just exchanging information about books.

One constant in the history of books is their power to take new forms, and to prompt new ways of reading as a result. Encountering those printed objects in all their variety may help us to worry less about the difference between print books and electronic books, but also to understand what's old and what's new about those worries. For each of the book's reinventions has prompted mixed, and strong, feelings. As cheap and portable print sold everywhere and read anytime replaced monumental volumes tethered to particular occasions, a new kind of object became a proxy for a new kind of self. That self could forge bonds with a long-dead author's mind, could make the book a stimulant or a sedative, a shield or a goad, a refuge or an arena. Show me how you want to read, and I'll show you who you want to be.

Chapter 1

READING OVER SHOULDERS

ONE SUMMER DAY in 2012, I trundled myself, a laptop, a phone, and a duffelful of paperbacks onto a south-bound train. I—we—were heading from Cambridge, Massa-chusetts, where I taught English literature, to New York, where I was hoping to examine one of the world's earliest vegetarian cookbooks. I snagged a seat in the Quiet Car in order to plunge into a novel, but the quiet proved short-lived. A few miles out-side Providence, a few chapters into *Middlemarch*, Mr. Casau-bon's cringe-making marriage proposal was interrupted by a loud command to "enjoy our library atmosphere."

In a year when real librarians were lugging microfiche read-ers to the curb and selling off card catalogs to conceptual artists, "library atmosphere" was a moving target. Amtrak's Northeast Corridor line opened its first Quiet Car in 2004, around the time when 3G broadband first enabled video streaming. This was also the year in which my own university began to debate the logistics of wheeling an ear-splitting coffee grinder up the ramp to its library coffee shop. Cast in the early twentieth century as a hushed radio-free zone and refashioned during the Cold War as a wholesome alternative to TV watching, "library" was now becoming the abracadabra that muted all cell phones.

Like libraries, trains house great books along with not-so-great reading matter. The commuter across from me ran a glazed eye over Amtrak's glossy in-house magazine: in it, a steakhouse ad juxtaposed bookshelves with hunting trophies. On the floor at the commuter's feet sprawled a catalog open to a full-page spread showing booklovers filling a new-and-improved Billy, Ikea's most ubiquitous bookshelf. In 2012, the thirty-something Billy was deepened, like a middle-aged man letting out his trousers,[1] from eleven inches (the depth of your average book) to fifteen inches (the dimensions of exhibition catalogs and tchotchkes). As the telephone conspired with photocopied takeout menus to reduce some mid-Manhattan ovens to shoe storage, digitization seemed to have turned bookshelves into curio cabinets.

Exiting the train, I passed a boutique hotel called The Library—another bid to scavenge public institutions for private atmosphere. Instead of room numbers, each suite bears a Dewey decimal number corresponding to the books that line its walls. Almost at the New York Public Library, I was stopped short by—could it really be—a bookstore? On a high-rent block off Fifth Avenue, the illusion couldn't last. A decorator in the window of an Anthropologie clothing boutique was busy posing T-shirts against a landscape of anatomically correct hand-distressed blank quartos, those large-format volumes that bear the same relation to a paperback-sized duodecimo as a wide-screen TV to an iPad mini. The same clothing chain, I later learned, was selling wallpaper printed with images of book spines—not a mail-order catalog in sight.[2]

Reaching the New York Public Library's central building, I lugged my laptop case up the most photogenic staircase in Manhattan. Since 2003, the NYPL has rented it out for events. After the heroine of the 2008 *Sex and the City* film chose that staircase as the scene of her abortive wedding, the starting price increased to $50,000. For an added fee, couples can request sculptures carved out of old books, or upgrade to card-catalog-style place cards in a room presided over by what a spokeswoman calls "real-life librarians."[3]

There's no point in specifying that something is "real" unless someone suspects that it's fake. When Amazon opened its first nonvirtual bookstore in 2015, a press release boasted of the shop's "real, wooden doors." (The punctuation, oddly, raises a question about the reality of the doors themselves, rather than just that of the wood.) In April 2017, 20 percent of surveyed Americans denied that ebooks were "real books."[4] The poll didn't specify what the antonym to "real" was. If ebooks are fake by virtue of possessing the function without the form (as some smokers say that e-cigarettes feel fake no matter how efficiently they deliver the nicotine), conversely some digital-age books keep the form while jettisoning the function.[5] No sooner did cell phones kill telephone books than ads popped up for the Boost, yellow foam shaped like a telephone book but sized for your toddler's behind.

As their contents drift online, books seem to be finding a new home on the coffee table. Far from displacing sewn or glued blocks of printed paper, the digital era seems to have invested those objects with new glamour. As pets get more pampering than farm animals, so long-form print is all the more treasured as it ceases to be the workhorse of our daily information gathering. To paraphrase Truman Capote: That's not reading. That's embalming.

———

Why this epidemic of Potemkin print? The most practical explanation is that readers—along with their e-readers—continue to be housed in rooms designed for earlier media. Built-in bookshelves are especially common in houses from the 1930s, when Edward Bernays, the father of public relations, lobbied architects on behalf of the publishing industry. Assuming that cabinetry would always generate demand for books, he didn't foresee that supply might outlast demand. As late as the 1950s, a writer in the *Library Quarterly* doubted that "changes in methods of reproducing the written word will have much effect on my cabinetmaker." He, for one, was confident that "the book for the mass-market will continue indefinitely to look like the book we know."[6]

Both men were proved wrong. As the advent of the scanner left filing cabinets sitting on curbs, so bookshelves threaten to become as purely decorative as candlesticks in a house lit by electricity. Where twentieth-century interior designers stashed TVs in clothes armoires and camouflaged keyboards in pencil drawers, twenty-first-century furniture manufacturers face, on the contrary, a surplus of furniture bearing the ghostly imprint of outdated objects. If the book is dying, its funeral appears to be open casket.

On the one hand, reports of the book's vulnerability; on the other, equally sweeping claims about books' power: just as books are everywhere and nowhere in midtown Manhattan storefronts, so Americans increasingly cast books at once as saviors and as martyrs. If that metaphor sounds hyperbolic, consider the outrage provoked by wounding books. At the dawn of the ebook era, in 2012, a reality-TV star garnered a couple thousand YouTube "dislikes" (a lot, in those innocent days) by taking an X-acto knife to a series of Lemony Snicket books. She proceeded (also on camera) to glue the severed spines together to make a decorative box. Recoiling from the craft project, one viewer testified, "I feel like I'm watching a murder."

The protesters weren't treating the book as a boat (however leaky) that ferries ideas from the author's brain to the reader's, or as an urn (however well wrought) into which large and durable ideas can be crammed for acid-free safekeeping. They were treating the book, instead, as a cue for certain actions (reading, not handling), certain attitudes (respecting, not repurposing), certain rules (look, don't touch).

There's nothing new about the urge to punish those who burn a Bible or a Quran. (To avoid the stigma surrounding destroying sacred texts altogether, Buddhists shred them to bulk out the walls of monasteries.[7]) Nor is there anything new about rules governing what not to do with a book, even, or especially, after it's passed its read-by date: the ethics and etiquette that dictate whether you can sit on a book, write in it, resell it, copy it, put a coffee cup on top of it, throw it away.

Before YouTube came on the scene, however, it would have seemed odd for a secular children's book to inspire an army of enforcers to wrest the vulnerable volumes back from the hands of others judged undeserving of custody. The viewers outraged by the hollowing out of Lemony Snicket volumes were protesting something new: the gutting of a once-vital medium. For them, a knifed book stood for the death of The Book, which in turn crystallized digital-era threats to the kind of self that reading had once engendered.

Digital-era readers were able to turn the book into such a symbol only because paperback-era readers had already forgotten the variety of forms that books had earlier taken and functions that they had earlier filled. Projecting backward the printed book's current definition as not-app erases a long history of what would only later come to be called "interactivity": readers underlined print, copied out passages, disbound books to arrange their pages in new orders. Universalizing the printed book's current function as not-database occludes how often readers have skipped and skimmed their way through print—browsing, searching, inking a homemade index into the endpapers. Treating the book as not-website renders invisible the overwhelming mass of printed books that have delivered soon-to-be-outdated practical information, rather than enduring wisdom.

When familiarity wanes, so does contempt. Once scarce and sacred objects, books entered everyday European life half a millennium ago thanks to paper (a portable and durable medium of which Europeans were late adopters) and print (which changed books from rarities to be worshipped to tools to be used). In restoring the printed book to a pedestal at the very moment when it's being shunted to the edges of everyday life, we circle back to the era when print looked like the latest newfangled gimmick.[8] Perhaps print is to digital as Madonna is to whore: we worship one but use the other.

The less we read texts, the more we look at books. And nowhere is that truer than on "Bookstagram," the corner of Instagram that spread-eagles books in the hands of a reader— always female, rarely clad in much more than a hand-crocheted scarf. Don't be fooled by their oops-you-caught-me postures: these young women are often on the payroll of a publishing house. Since 2014, Bookstagram has outstripped more purely verbal social media as a promotional tool.[9] Bookstagram celebrity Anabel Jimenez @inthebookcorner reported that her most popular posts were "unboxing"videos. Each showed her unpacking the hauls that publishers send her, sometimes with comments on the looks of the covers involved: "I'm seeing a trend of blue going on."[10] The savviest bookstagrammers light the scene with the help of Lisa Smith, a lifelong booklover whose vision began to fade after the onset of rheumatoid arthritis. Smith's way to "keep alive . . . my love for literature": a small business selling scented candles. Some of her wares are book themed (choose between leather-tinged Lost in the Stacks or coffee-and-chai Bookstore), others text themed (amber-scented Heathcliff candle or floral Jane Eyre).[11] Books sell. That is, they sell things other than books.

Like candles, books have come to stand for the past—one less efficient than an electric light, the other less efficient than an electronic device, both therefore more atmospheric. But what exactly is the modernity against which these antiques provide a bulwark? One answer lies in Ray Bradbury's short story "Exchange." In this 1996 tribute to libraries, a veteran returns to his hometown to find that all of his childhood acquaintances have moved on. Only the local branch remains as he remembers it, with its faithful female staffer playing Penelope to the hero's Odysseus. "Librarians save everything," the prodigal reflects: "save" in the sense of "redeem," but also "save" as in "preserve," even "hoard."[12]

"Exchange" was written in Bradbury's subterranean home office, but his writing career began in a more public basement, the typewriter room deep below UCLA's Powell Library. (After the author's death enabled a developer to bulldoze the house, fans at Indiana University re-created the home office brick by brick and book by book.) The libraries that Bradbury called his "nesting place" offered more literal protection during the Cold War, when public safety officials requisitioned them as atomic fallout shelters.[13]

The nostalgia registered in "Exchange" typifies a moment when bytes, rather than bombs, were the threat from which readers needed shelter. This time, they huddled in libraries but also in the idea of the age-old printed book. In 2011, an otherwise sweeping history of media revolutions posited that "one format has remained virtually unchanged until recently: the book."[14] A few years later, an otherwise edgy art catalog declared that "the codex has sat like an anchored boat as the seas of change wash all around it but don't affect it."[15] And at around the same time, a psycho-oncologist running a reading group for Sloan-Kettering told me that "you need your three-year-old to teach you how to operate your new phone, but books are the same as they have always been." Where book historians use printed matter to uncover history, these booklovers use print to stop time in its tracks.

In 2018, journalist Susan Orlean opened her punningly titled *The Library Book* by evoking her memory of reading rooms. Even stepping into an unfamiliar branch transports her back, in her imagination, to the library that cocooned her childhood. "Nothing had changed—there was the same soft tsk-tsk-tsk of pencil on paper, and the muffled murmuring. . . . The scarred wooden checkout counters, and the librarians' desks, as big as boats, and the bulletin board, with its fluttering, raggedy notices, were all the same."[16] Orlean's point is not that libraries are invulnerable. On the contrary, the history introduced by Orlean's autobiographical vignette centers on a fire in the Los Angeles Central Library's main branch that in 1986 destroyed half a million books, including the complete works of Ray Bradbury. But the fragility of books is counterpoised, in Orlean's account, by the illusion that libraries stop the clock, returning adults to a different era and a more innocent self.

Even scholars have joined the rush to cast the book as a bolt-hole. Ever since Sven Birkerts titled his 1994 book *The Gutenberg Elegies: The Fate of Reading in an Electronic Age*, a growing stack of titles have cast reading as out of step with their own present. Consider David Ulin's *The Lost Art of Reading: Why Books Matter in a Distracted Time* (2010), Alan Jacobs's *The Pleasures of Reading in an Age of Distraction* (2011), David Mikics's *Slow Reading in a Hurried Age* (2013), Martha Pennington and Robert Waxler's *Why Reading Books Still Matters: The Power of Literature in Digital Times* (2017), and Meghan Cox Gurdon's *The Enchanted Hours: The Miraculous Power of Reading Aloud in the Age of Distraction* (2019). You'll have noticed that the "in" around which each title pivots counterpoints reading to an "age" or a "time." While each book links the decline of reading to a different category of problem—political (Ulin), spiritual (Jacobs), moral (Mikics), social (Pennington and Waxler), or developmental (Gurdon)—all ask reading to counteract not just the problems that characterize their moment in history but also, more fundamentally, the very fact of historical change.

———

A longer view suggests, on the contrary, that printed books have consistently been the newest of media. Far from providing a refuge from history, books make history—not just through the ideas they vehicle, but also through the technologies created for manufacturing and distributing them. Printed books have been the newest of media, beginning in the century following the invention of movable type, when they became the first truly standardized good. While late-medieval manuscripts circulated through something approaching a market (they weren't always produced, as we would say today, "on demand"), each copy of a manuscript differed slightly from every other. A buyer of a printed book, in contrast, could know exactly what he or (occasionally) she was getting: see one copy, seen them all.

Because that standardization made it possible for books to be branded and advertised at a time when most objects were handmade and locally sold, print blazed the way for forms of marketing that would later spread to patent medicines, then to pretty much everything else. By the nineteenth century, as historian Ted Striphas has demonstrated, books became the first consumer goods marketed specifically as gifts, and the first to be sold on consumer credit.[17] Books counteracted the moral stigma of debt, because reading (or at least reading weighty tomes, rather than newspapers and supposedly trashy fiction) could be rebranded as a virtuous investment of time rather than a frivolous self-indulgence. Along with pianos, those multi-volume encyclopedias without which (advertisers warned) no house would be a home paved the way for a credit economy that would eventually extend to everything from layaway for clothes to subprime mortgages for houses.

Books were also the first goods to be made what we would now call "browsable," because bookstores were the first to display their wares on self-service shelves rather than safely behind the counter.[18] In the 1940s, one of the first businesses to pipe in Muzak was Barnes and Noble—a bookstore that, a few decades later, became one of the first chains to advertise on national TV. As publishing entrepreneur Richard Nash explains, far from being "dragged kicking and screaming into each new area of capitalism . . . books not only are part and parcel of consumer capitalism, they virtually began it."[19]

Behind the scenes, meanwhile, printed books long drove changes in the objects and protocols used to keep track of merchandise. Books blazed the way for paper packaging and printed labeling. The first barcodes, as Striphas points out, were slapped onto books.[20] (Just as ride-hailing apps preceded driverless cars, so inventory control systems had preceded e-texts.) The book's long history at the forefront of inventory control makes it unsurprising that when a young entrepreneur named Jeff Bezos needed a guinea pig for a new online sales system, the obvious choice was books.

Printed books, as Striphas and Nash show, were cutting-edge technologies. Yet in one 2013 Scholastic survey, one out of two parents preferred print books on the grounds that "they give the child a break from technology."[21] In Amazon's hometown, the Seattle Public Library pioneered the soon-to-be-ubiquitous idea of a "technology-free reading room."[22] If you've read this far, you'll have noticed that those statements are oxymorons.

Two decades after his *Gutenberg Elegies*, Birkerts returned to the question of how new technologies were changing the "process of reading traditional—literary—books in the traditional way." But the technologies by which books were printed and exchanged have always been as various as the uses to which readers (or just would-be readers) put them. Asking "can the literary survive technology?" Birkerts might as well have asked whether fish can survive water.[23] Technologies have always generated some literary forms while making others unimaginable— whether the tool in question was a chisel or a typewriter. And literature has always been shaped by the tug-of-war between material objects that can be bought or borrowed, shelved or held, and experiences that unfold only in readers' brains.

If printed matter is no less subject to commercial and technological change than electronic devices, conversely ebooks depend just as much on physical infrastructures ranging from server farms to cell-phone towers. One journalist complained recently that "virtual books, like virtual holidays or virtual relationships, are not real."[24] Fair enough. But neither are the images conjured up by blobs of ink on pressed wood pulp. Books in whatever medium connect us with fictional characters, with dead or distant authors, and with fellow readers who may be distant in time (like the ones we meet via pencil scrawls in a library book), or in space (as with the other readers whose highlighting we see in an ebook or the hands flipping the same paperback bestseller, across the street or across the globe).

The crucial difference, I'm suggesting, may not be between print and digital but rather among the different uses to which readers put text, whatever its physical form. Faced with the question of what counts as a book, linguist Naomi Baron recently reflected that "for more than 1,500 years, the answer was simple: a collection of pages with writing (or pictures) on them, bound together.... You could smell its binding. Admire it on a shelf. Lend it to a friend. Lose it. Burn it."[25]

Book historians, in contrast, emphasize that, for most of those 1,500 years, the rules of engagement with books were anything but simple. Some books weren't meant to be lent: a pocket-sized almanac printed with holiday dates and astrological information went everywhere its owner did, as personal to a single user as any smartphone. Other books weren't made to be lost: only a monster would replace the family Bible with a crisper copy, let alone (as in Baron's example) burn it. Still others, like novels, spent the first centuries of their life being hidden in a drawer rather than admired on a shelf.

Schoolchildren of my generation were not supposed to paw or inhale—let alone lose—the books that we were lent by a school district. And Cold War–era paperbacks have rarely been sniffed (if anything, users held their noses from the cheap glue). At the other extreme, illiterate Victorian vegetable vendors eyeballed and touched old newspapers to assess their weight and texture. They weren't in the market for absorbing reading material; what they wanted was absorbent paper, to mop up spills.[26]

When we put books under a microscope rather than on a pedestal, we come to realize that what all printed books have in common is variety—across historical periods and even within a single culture. They come in different sizes and shapes (a hefty coffee-table book vs. a dainty pocket diary), are bound to their owners for different periods of time (a family Bible passed down from generation to generation or a textbook loaned to another student for the year), invite or at least allow different uses (reading or wrapping).

Those differences form one topic of the course on book history that I've taught at Harvard for the past two decades. As photocopied course listings gave way to websites and apps, I found comfort in returning every September to an unchanging game. The night before class, I raid my son's craft supplies for a roll of tape and a ream of construction paper to wrap the covers and spines of a dozen books like some amateurish Christo. I fish the anonymized books out of my backpack one by one, asking the students to identify each. Someone always spots the yellow pages thanks to their color, and even a generation reared on spell-check recognizes a thumb index. The pink fore edges and silk ribbon give away a leather-bound pocket King James Bible, and frequent hotel-goers spot a Gideon's spongy shine.

On the last day of the semester, we return to the game that one student dubbed Name That Book—but now, we meet in the library. This time, instead of pasting over the covers, students take turns wrapping a dish towel around their eyes. Each has a chance to stumble to the wall, blindman's-bluff-like, to pull down a volume at random, and to take twenty questions from the rest of the class.

How much friction does your hand encounter when it runs along the page? Which surfaces are slipperiest, which pages noisiest? (Plates sandwiched in the middle scream biography; the tissue paper that covers illustrations has a different "rattle," as the technical term goes, than printed paper.) Where in the book do the edges feel sharpest? (Monographs crisp progressively as readers lose interest, but students recognize reference books by the limp pages periodically punctuating unread neighbors.) Will the book stay open as you take notes, or are two hands needed to flatten the page spread? Does it seem to be bound for posterity or for the trash can?

Name That Book jolts students who love losing themselves in an imaginary universe back into an awareness of their own physical surroundings, beginning with the sight and sound and feel of the object in their hands. English majors are used to being coaxed to do (as our ugly phrase goes) the reading. Being asked *not* to read frustrates some and outrages others.

For all their itching to unbind their eyes and unwrap the books, though, the students who are the angriest at the start often prove by the end of class the most skilled at describing what the exercise taught them. Prevented from seeing through the physical object to the words it contains, they become curious about the people and machines that manufactured it, the individuals and organizations that sold or gave it away, the librarians who placed it on now-dusty shelves, the backpacks in which it was once carried, and the fingers that wore down its pages.

Naming is actually the least of what the students end up doing—now, or when we rip off the blindfold. More important, they're picking up on what mixed signals any book gives about how and where and why to use it. Seeing the book as a technology means understanding it not just as a statement about the world outside its pages, but as a set of instructions about how those pages themselves should be handled and read. Blindfolded, each student begins to notice conflicts between the stories that a book tells, the story that a title page and copy-right page tell about a book, and the stories that the look and feel and smell of the book tell about its users.

In looking at books instead of looking through them, my students aren't acting as literary critics (though some of them are English majors) or historians of ideas (though reverse psychology ensures that some will become curious about the ideas censored by construction paper). Rather, they are trying out the academic discipline that emerged during the Cold War under the name of book history.

Book historians study inscribed objects. That can mean long-form print, but despite their name, book historians have extended their remit to manuscripts, newspapers, even posters and tombstones. Some, called bibliographers, focus on the transmission of texts. (These texts can be electronic: one of the field's most prominent scholars, Matthew Kirschenbaum, specializes in the history of word processing.) Some are more interested in the people who make these objects (whether that means authors or printers or publishers); others, in the people who circulate them (whether that means bookstore workers or librarians); still others, in the people who read them. Some book historians, like me, hail from English departments or other national literatures. Others find their way to the field from history departments, others from art history or the history of science, and others from libraries and schools of information science. However different our training, we all seek to make sense of the relation between words and things.

Book history emerged within universities at the very moment when the general public was losing interest in the book's material properties. Around the time of World War II, the paperback reprint ushered in an age of treating instantiations of a single text as interchangeable: same wine, different bottles. Literary critics abandoned book sniffing to collectors with more money than sense and bibliographic description to underpaid and undervalued lady librarians. Today, increasing numbers of English professors like me are beginning once again to have opinions and feelings about the provenance of the glass and the layout of the cellars. Or, in artist and scholar Amaranth Borsuk's lovely metaphor, "rather than offering up a crystal goblet" into which words can be poured, digital-era approaches to reading "invite us to trace our finger along text's rim and make it sing."[27]

Different eras, these changes suggest, don't just produce different kinds of books. Each also generates new ways of treating books—more specifically, new assumptions about what aspects of these physical objects deserve readers' attention. When my students notice how different an eighteenth-century sermon collection looks from a twentieth-century airport paperback, the difference between a laminated chemistry textbook and the electronic version on their laptop begins to look less unprecedented. In the other direction, though, they begin to see that electronic technologies are in fact creating something radically new. Digital tools may not be upending our reading practices any more drastically than changing forms of print did. What they are revolutionizing is our ideas *about* reading. In the process, they're remaking the printed past.

Book historians focus on a fact that print users began to forget once the medium became familiar enough to ignore: that a book (whether printed or electronic) is something more than just a bucket into which ideas can be crammed for convenient carrying from an author to a reader. A book dies on the shelf (or the server) unless it's also a prompt for gestures, a catalyst of mental operations and emotional states, a badge of a reader's or even just an owner's identity.

Book historians can recognize ourselves in the defenders of Lemony Snicket. We share their commitment to material objects, over and above the words that they contain. The difference is that we preserve books not as a bulwark against history, but as a witness to it.

As the blindfolded students learn from Name That Book, literary critics focus on the *texts* we read, while book historians focus on the *books* that we touch or smell or weigh in our hands, gauging which will lie flat when we need our hands to eat a sandwich, or which will fit best in a particular pocket. Literary critics interpret the stories that books tell; book historians tell stories about the objects that contain them. Book historians' heroes and villains are the publishers who commissioned the book, the rag-and-bone dealers who scavenged the linen underwear that was pulped to make its pages, the censors who withdrew it from circulation, the smugglers who backpacked it across a border, and sometimes even the scholars who granted a second life to a piece of printed matter by enthroning it on their syllabus.

Others' love is easy to dismiss as perversion. Some book historians caricature literary critics as ostrich-like idealists, willfully ignoring the human beings who produced and transmitted the sequence of words with which they commune unmediated. Some literary critics dismiss book historians as idiots savants who either sniff bindings without understanding the words they contain, or recite obsessive statistics about tons of wood pulp.

When I wear my literary critic's hat I focus on clumps of words, while when I wear my book historian's hat I'm more interested in tangible objects. In practice, though, any scholar does both. In fact, even readers who aren't scholars tend to toggle between awareness of the *text* and the *book*. Amazon customers are reviewing the text when they give *David Copperfield* four and a half stars for its "insight into the human condition"; they're reviewing the book when they note "great price, good condition" but downgrade to three stars because "there's a substantial blank area at the bottom of every page, so that the print could have been made much larger while maintaining the page count."[28]

To grasp the point of distinguishing *books* from *texts*, think back to those students who spotted the onionskin pages of the pocket King James Bible in an instant but sat stumped when confronted with a paperback reprint of the same translation. Same *text*, different *books*: the very same sequence of words means something different—*does* something different—depending on whether it's made for a desk or a pocket, a classroom or a church. Comparing these two editions of the same text makes visible how much of our reaction to a book is shaped by factors other than the words it contains. Its look and feel and smell instruct us wordlessly in how and why to read it—alone or in company, in search of learning or of salvation.

Nor does *Pride and Prejudice* mean the same thing whether it reaches its readers in the form of a paper-covered first edition signed only "by the author of Sense and Sensibility," or the form of a Philadelphia publisher who shifted emphasis by retitling his 1832 reprint *Elizabeth Bennet: Or, Pride and Prejudice*, or of a BBC tie-in paperback, or of a machine-read, volunteer-proofread text uploaded to an ad-supported Ukrainian website for pirated music.

Why stop at multiple editions of the same text? Even two copies of the same edition can take on different meanings. Toni Morrison opens her novel *God Help the Child* with the narrator observing that when her parents went to the courthouse to get married,

> there were two Bibles, and they had to put their hands on the one reserved for Negroes. The other one was for white people's hands. The Bible! Can you beat it? My mother was a house-keeper for a rich white couple. They ate every meal she cooked and insisted she scrub their backs while they sat in the tub, and God knows what other intimate things they made her do, but no touching of the same Bible.[29]

In the antebellum American South, states had passed laws forbidding enslaved men and women from reading out of fear of the dangerous messages expressed in prose. During Reconstruction, in contrast, bigots worried that sharing books across racial lines created undesirable bonds. In 1889, for example, North Carolina legislated that "books shall not be interchangeable between the white and colored schools, but shall continue to be used by the race first using them." For these lawmakers as for Morrison's characters, the meaning of the book didn't just lie in its words. Where a volume was kept, who was allowed to read it, and who was expected only to dust it sent a signal about the worth of the human beings who touched it. And that signal could contradict or even outweigh the more explicit message about the worth of all believers that the text of the Bible in *God Help the Child* contained.

Tracing across different cultures the shifting division of labor between the text (a series of words) and the book (a tangible thing) helps book historians understand reading as an out-of-body experience but also a complex coordination between the eyes that see the letters, the neck that cranes over its pages, the hands that hold the volume open. Disentangling timeless ideas from time-bound objects shows texts freeing readers from their surroundings but books anchoring readers more firmly within them. And tracing the networks of readers who sold, loaned, recommended, or even withheld books shows book historians how crucial middlemen and middlewomen are to the tête-à-tête between reader and author.

You wouldn't have opened this book if you weren't a passionate reader. And if you've made it as far as this page, you may even belong to that part of the population that takes an English course or ten. Odds are that you have strong opinions about poems and essays and novels, and even stronger feelings. But if you're not one of the few booklovers lucky enough to staff a circulation desk or stock a bookstore or amass a collection, you may not be in the habit of thinking about wood pulp, ink, and glue.

I didn't used to. I've always loved to read. But until adolescence brought competing forms of connection, I also read to love. First that meant loving words, then loving literary characters, then loving an imagined author, and loving the other people who had loved all of those things. And while many people I knew wanted to have read books, I never wanted to get over the delicious moment of being in the middle of reading them.

Yet, long as I've loved texts, I came later to loving books. I didn't begin to notice paper or glue until my imaginative life moved in to someone else's bookshelves. In my teens, my family moved five times—five countries, five sublets, and five sets of bookshelves. Today, I own only a few books from before college (Grimm's fairy tales, minus a Maurice Sendak illustration torn out in terror; a *Joy of Cooking* penciled by my mother; and, reader, I carried *Jane Eyre*). But the disappearance of a year's worth of reading into yard sales every July meant that every August brought new opportunities for bibliomancy. Puzzling over which paperbacks inhabited which room in each new apartment, filling each landlord's pre-scratched saucepan with the ingredients underlined in some stranger's cookbook with some stranger's pencil, I was already being primed to read over others' shoulders.

My security blanket was the library—or more precisely, that far-flung web of standardized call numbers known as the US library system. Even as the books that I had owned ended up on curbs or in storage lockers, the same titles popped up, with reassuring familiarity, in the same order on the same Dewey decimal 800 shelves in libraries approached by the same Andrew Carnegie–approved grand staircases. No frigate like a book, Emily Dickinson wrote; reading transported her from the house in which she sat for twenty years. But when your own surroundings yaw, books feel more like an anchor.

In college, the library remained more tempting than the bookstore: no incentive to lug books or boards and cinder blocks from walk-up to walk-up every August. But then, I won the academic's closest equivalent to the lottery. My tenure-track job— at the turn of the millennium, they still existed—came with an ID that swiped me into a 17-million-volume library. Or more precisely, into a redbrick building containing the most popular 3 million or so of those; the rest shivered in a climate-controlled off-site depository.

At home, I ventured to buy. My first purchases were paperback, then cloth, finally the occasional coffee-table book along with the eponymous furniture. The sublets gave way to a lease, a lease to a mortgage, Ikea bookcases whose fiberboard was chipped from too many U-Hauls to built-ins that weren't going anywhere. Now I was the one whose books were being pawed by the occasional renter when I went away for a year. I'd return to find a book out of place and speculate about why the stranger I'd met when handing over the keys would have pulled that particular volume off the shelf.

The U-Haul had hauled me to a bookish town. At dusk, one bow window after another displaying Billy bookshelves glowed as eye-catchingly as Amsterdam sex shops. From a distance, Ikea seemed to have issued them preloaded. I could recognize here the black spine of a Routledge Reader, there the orange of an older Penguin. But then books, too, are mass-produced multiples. In both cases, I realized, standardization opens the way to personalization: as we each slot a slightly different combination of books onto the identical fiberboard shelves, so we each dog-ear different pages.

On trash day, sidewalks disgorged introductions to psycho-analysis. In the local laundromat, I learned to match each washer setting to a genre: the short spin for synthetics meant an essay in one of the *New Yorkers* that a neighbor had placed there after jaggedly scissoring out his or her address label, while the long soak needed by bed linens gave me an excuse to read a waterlogged police procedural that I'd never have borrowed from a more official library. After a few years of speculating about whose piled-up clothes corresponded to whose aban-doned paperbacks, though, we bought our own washer-dryer. No more glimpses of the neighbors' books along with the neighbors' spinning underwear.

From a booklover, I became a literary critic; from a literary critic, a book historian. As I changed from a nosy sublet-er to a card-carrying English professor to a roving book historian, I also went from seeing printed paper as reams that had to be schlepped up and down stairs, to vehicles that delivered words to me as trucks haul gravel, to witnesses that told a story about the human beings who made and used and shared them.

Book historians aren't the only people who believe that a book can tell us something about the hands that held it or the eyes that scanned its pages. Take the tradition of swearing in to a political office on a volume that belonged to some famous predecessor. In January 2017, our new president took oath on the bibliographic equivalent of a Whopper, a two-Bible stack in which a Sunday-school graduation gift embossed with his own name sat on top of Abraham Lincoln's copy, still in its presentation box.

Trump was dragging into the selfie age Barack Obama's swearing in on that very same copy of Lincoln's Bible, augmented in Obama's second inauguration by the copy that Martin Luther King Jr. had used for travel. Rare-book dealers call such books "association copies"—objects whose value derives not just from their rarity or beauty or age, but also from the identity of their past owners. It's hard to imagine future officials reusing the iPad on whose Bible app Atlantic City firefighters were sworn in when the official in charge misplaced his leatherette Bible.[30]

Presidents leave a paper trail. Trump explained, on the record, that he didn't read because "I'm always busy doing a lot."[31] (But what if reading also counted as doing?) And then there's the external evidence. No sooner had Trump been inaugurated, after all, than a photo of his bookshelves was leaked. On them faced outward—more like a bookstore display than a library shelf—multiple copies of his own oeuvre, or rather the oeuvre of his now-disgruntled ghostwriters.[32] An earlier politician, British prime minister Benjamin Disraeli, had at least churned out twenty-odd of his own when he declared that "[if] I want to read a book, I write one."[33] All this ensures that we know more about Trump's reading (or lack thereof) than we do for the vast majority of Americans, past or present.

But most books, like many readers, end up in unmarked graves. And paradoxically, this often holds truest for the books that during their lifetimes were the best loved. Enter the reading room of Harvard's Houghton Library and you'll be encircled by countless volumes of now-unreadable eighteenth-century sermons whose snow-white pages seem never to have been touched, let alone read. What you won't find is a copy of the first edition of *The New England Primer* (1687–1690), the single most popular book in seventeenth- and eighteenth-century America after the Bible.

It's not just Harvard: nowhere in the world today can you find a copy of the *Primer* published before 1727, because they were handled to pieces before any librarian thought to collect them. Only from the indirect evidence of publishers' advertisements, and from one surviving scrap of a page that someone tore off to stiffen the binding of another book, do we know that the *Primer* had by that time been printed in several hundred thousand copies.

One challenge of book history, therefore, is to glean from the clues stashed in library stacks some hint about the imaginative lives of people who never left a written—let alone printed—spoor. When scholars get lucky, we manage to unearth a diary or a letter in which someone names the book that touched or enraged her. But most of the time, we have to make do with a patchwork of contradictory dead ends. And even copious marginal notes don't always reflect rapt reading. Until the advent of untaxed wood-pulp paper in the second half of the nineteenth century, printed books were valued in large part for the blank writing surfaces they offered. With no scrap paper lying around, books formed the most convenient place to scribble a shopping list or to practice one's signature (particularly common in books owned by children). Printed books could also become repositories for handwritten information about their owners. Family Bibles were the obvious place to record births and deaths, but at the beginning of the nineteenth century American physician Benjamin Waterhouse used his, more daringly, to record the dates of children's and servants' smallpox vaccinations.

Lacking words, scholars like me make do with negative evidence. Do ink stains, drink stains, or even traces of candle wax and smoke betray which pages lay open the longest? Which books have been handled to pieces, which gathered dust on a shelf? An unintended consequence of embossing technology is that Braille books reveal wear and tear more reliably than does ordinary printing. One 1939 study of schools for blind African American children revealed that books handed down from schools for white children had "dots . . . so worn down as to be all but indistinguishable."[34]

Even the absence of damage tells a story of its own. Hemingway professed to love his friend Joyce's novel *Ulysses*, but his copy survives crisp and clean to this day, with only the first and last pages cut.[35] Objects confess truths that readers' diaries and letters and reviews do their best to hide. Books catch their readers out in fibs, because reading—or non-reading, as seems to have been Hemingway's case—is one of the most private things we do. Perhaps Hemingway should have used the service devised by the Irish humorist Flann O'Brien, who proposed (tongue in cheek) that homeowners decorating their living rooms with books bought by the yard should also outsource the breaking in of the volumes to a professional "bookhandler" who would crack spines and apply coffee stains to strategically chosen pages.[36]

Such staging feels worse, somehow, than when realtors insert champagne bottles in the fridge. Book ethics isn't just a set of rules about whether and how to give books a decent burial. It also includes the rules about when it's okay to lie, or to make books lie for and about you. And that question has often been social as much as moral. A *New York Times* writer sniffed in 1878 that "furniture, piano-fortes, pictures, may be bought by order in a week, but books in any noticeable number, which seem to belong in the rooms where they are found, must be the result of accumulation. Their rows are the tree-avenues which mark the residence of the aristocracy of mental culture."[37] Like the woods rooted on a landed estate, books vouched for an ancestral pedigree.

Even when they're not bearing false witness, books can send mixed messages. Preserving a volume in spotless Mylar can express love for a book; so can cracking its spine and interleaving its pages with wisps of toilet paper. But over the past few centuries, respect has diverged from love. In Shakespeare's time, readers were not just permitted but expected to annotate. Schoolmasters taught boys elaborate notational systems for use in the margins. Book historian William Sherman found one seventeenth-century reader filling a margin with a neat drawing of his own finger pointing to a key passage, down to an anatomically correct nail.[38] To read implied to write. Nor did that writing have to take the form of ink or easily erased pencil. Pricking your name into the endpapers with a needle seems to have counted as housewifely virtue, judging from the carefully spaced dots that mark "A. Evans" in one copy of a 1756 abridgment of Samuel Richardson's great novel *Pamela*. Narrated by a maid who writes letters home when she should be embroidering her master's waistcoat, the novel shows that master resisting ordinary women's insistence on leaving a mark. "You mind your Pen more than your Needle," he tells Pamela in between attempts to rape her; "I don't want such idle Sluts to stay in my house."[39] A. Evans, however, seems to have seen the pen as interchangeable with the needle, making writing in books as laudably industrious as embroidering initials on the family's linen.

In the following generation, however, Romanticism fostered readers eager to be marked by texts, not to leave their literal mark. An etiquette in which the best gift was a book bearing the marks of the giver's pencil (pre-owned, as we say today, but also pre-underlined) gave way to one in which the ideal book was pristine, the ideal reader hands-off. The public libraries that began to spread in England and America after 1850 placed scribbling in books under the same taboo as scratching your initials into the bathroom wall.

Good reading, once defined by what you did to a book, now became a matter of what you refrained from doing. Like Smokey Bear, teachers now enjoined schoolchildren to leave books as clean as they found them. In Britain, the 1910 prohibition on kissing Bibles in court coincided with libraries' investment in "book fumigators" invented to protect their patrons from each other's germs.[40] On the first page of Maurice Sendak's 1963 classic *Where the Wild Things Are*, Max's naughtiness is wordlessly conveyed by his position, standing on top of a stack of books. To grow up means learning not to Pat the Bunny.

In twentieth-century books, this hands-off stance leaves articulate, relevant marginalia few and far between. Even more rarely does one find such articulate comments responding to other articulate comments. One exception lies in the marks that two successive Harvard University Library users have left in the margin of a 1953 copy of Rollo May's highbrow self-help book *Man's Search for Himself*, where a penciled "that's me" next to the printed explanation that "aliveness often means the capacity ... to be creatively idle" is annotated in turn in a different handwriting declaring that "I'd really like to meet the person who did all these underlinings and comments and see if he or she found what he was looking for."[41] A dialogue between author and reader gives way here to a three-way conversation. Such conversations, however, were coming to look as inconsiderate as talking in the library. By the time I entered college in the late 1980s, my friends and I scorned those few classmates who remained selfish enough to blaze a trail through library-owned textbooks with their yellow highlighters, like cats marking intellectual territory.

As online commenting proliferates, though, the tide is beginning to turn again. The frequency of readers' annotations on texts may turn out to look something like a reverse bell curve. The heaviest annotations come before and after a twentieth-century blip when marginalia went underground. Perhaps books will once more bear witness to the mental and emotional lives of their readers.

In the meantime, Victorianists like me shoot jealous glances at the well-scribbled pages in front of the sixteenth-century-ists sitting one library desk over. The later your texts, the thinner the record of reader response. The Victorians didn't just bind themselves to look without touching; they also amassed "career library books" that passed from cradle to grave in libraries from which drink or even ink were excluded.[42] The result, ironically enough, is that I encountered beaten and dirtied books more often in the world's great research libraries than in my (great, in a different way) local branch.

One day early in the twenty-first century, the New York Public Library's overflowing online catalog led me to the Pforzheimer Collection, whose wood-paneled walls hold early-nineteenth-century volumes obsessively (and expensively) amassed by an early-twentieth-century investment banker. Curator Liz Denlinger arranged in front of me, as deftly as an expert hostess setting a table, the pair of protective foam wedges known in rare-book libraries as a "cradle." Into its fold, draped with a sticky green felt that you might recognize from card tables, she snuggled a volume that was anything but newborn.

Vegetable Cookery; with an Introduction, Recommending Abstinence from Animal food and Intoxicating Liquors, by "a Lady," was dated 1833; the catalog told me that it was the fourth edition of a volume first published in England in 1821. Baked rice omelet, macaroni omelet, tapioca omelet; the seventeen recipes for pea soup squelched the hunger that had nagged me since rushing past the panini stalls dotting Bryant Park. But *Vegetable Cookery* turned out to be a remarkable book, and not just because no one in Europe had ever before thought to compile a cookbook without a single recipe for what the introduction (invoking the authority of a certain Dr. Lambe) termed "the bodies of animals in nearly all states of disease." Collected from a series of pamphlets, it had a claim to be considered the first vegetarian cookbook in English.

Compared to any literary genre, cookbooks are steady sellers—and greater innovators, if you look for innovation in the form of marketing strategies rather than narrative techniques. Recipe books were among the first genres to adopt print. (The diet manual *De honesta voluptate* [1474] appeared only two decades after the Gutenberg Bible.) They went on to pioneer installment publication (*Vegetable Cookery* being a case in point), monthly subscription clubs, and paid product placement. In the last century, cookbooks were early adopters of laminated pages and photographic illustrations. In ours, they were one of the first genres to drift online via a welter of competing recipe apps.

I was surprised to notice, though, that *Vegetable Cookery* clung to one strangely mismatched tradition. Its rag-paper pages were clad, Crusoe-like, in skin flayed from a goat. In the early years of printing, most sheets were sold loose; the end user could then customize the final book by choosing his own binding, much as we personalize smartphones with our choice of plastic "skin." By the nineteenth century, this practice had begun to change: books were commonly sold pre-bound. But cloth and leather covers were only slowly giving way to paper. In 1900 alone, Oxford University Press's binderies bought the skins of 100,000 animals, mainly for Bibles. Around the same time, a British and Foreign Bible Society catalog offered readers a whole menagerie of covers artificially grained to resemble the skins of different animals: match your Bible to your Sunday shoes.

The inside of *Vegetable Cookery* was made of a different animal. Every page of this rebuke to the "flesh-consuming community" was coated with a sizing boiled down from horse bones, replaced only a century later by synthetic chemicals. Its tips about how to replace steak with sago soup and breadcrumb pie were printed on carcasses. I usually imagine books as products of a person's mind, not an animal's body. But what was left of my appetite disappeared when I realized that the library in which I was sitting was a graveyard. Just as the condition of Hemingway's *Ulysses* contradicted his words, so the raw materials of *Vegetable Cookery* tugged against its plea for humans to live without taking the lives of other animals.

I wondered who had written this strange volume, and luckily, a penciled annotation had outed the modestly anonymized "Lady." The title page was signed "Florence Lee," and in the same handwriting as the signature, the book's erstwhile owner had added "Mrs. Brotherton wife of Joseph Brotherton Esq. M.P. for Salford—." A detour back to the *Dictionary of National Biography*'s calfskin-bound volumes informed me that Joseph was a minister of the radical Cowherdite Bible Christian sect. A teetotaler as well as a vegetarian, Joseph supported public libraries in the hope that they would draw working-class men away from the other place where you could find shelter, warmth, and news: the pub. On Mrs. Brotherton herself, except for a first name and a tentative birthdate, the *DNB* remained as silent as the title page.

At a time when increasing numbers of books have been digitized by the badly paid human scanners whose latex-clad thumbs make the occasional cameo in the corner of a Google Books page, Victorianists rarely set sail for unknown libraries unless we're fishing for something more than the printed text alone. Harvard owns another copy of *Vegetarian Cookery*, shelved in the medical school library among textbooks gathering dust now that PubMed can be accessed from any password-equipped premed's smartphone. But pages that a dealer could honestly advertise as mint condition proclaim Harvard's copy to be a career library book.

The NYPL's copy, in contrast, is a used book. Florence Lee's thumb wasn't gloved when she turned the pages. Sticky from the Cheeto-coating-textured dust that rubs off old leather, my own fingers encounter batter, butter, and some transparent stain whose composition I will myself not to identify—shortening? Saliva? The corner of one particularly unhinged page hints that the arrowroot pudding may have been finger-lickin' good.

If you're a cook, you may have used stains as a kind of improvised heat map, opening a recipe book first at the stuck-together pages that provide an unintentional vote of confidence in an often-made dish. Handling can remake a book as decisively as can words penciled in the margins. In both cases, readers refuse to remain silent consumers; the book becomes their story, remade in their image. When a woman-handled book betrays the confidences of long-dead readers, the find makes up for months of dead ends.

Yet the vast majority of data about reading today is no longer painstakingly hand gathered by human gleaners like me. Seeing analytics accumulate second by second in the grasp of businesses like Google and Amazon, a scholar who's spent years reading over long-dead shoulders in dusty libraries can feel like a pedestrian who sees a bus whiz along the road she's been trudging, splashing her with mud into the bargain.

Even for analytics-grubbing Silicon Valley, though, to know what people read—or even where, when, at what pace—isn't to know why. No matter how many keystrokes you track and blinks you time, others' reading remains as hard to peer into as others' hearts.

Chapter 2

THE REAL LIFE OF BOOKS

A RECENT *NEW YORK TIMES* article describes a Soho shop "that could be mistaken for an haute bachelor pad. . . . It's supposed to be organic, like a home. Clients roam around, they hang out." In the digital age, the journalist gushes, the information that clients need can be accessed more cheaply online: the only way to sell the older technology is through personal recommendations and events that create a sense of community. You might be forgiven for assuming, as I did on first glance, that the product in question was books. No: it's analog watches.[1]

The book isn't the only object whose old-fashioned version becomes more glamorous as electronic equivalents replace it day to day. If buying an analog Rolex gives the same thrill of stepping off the conveyor belt of history as does buying a hefty hardback, then perhaps the resilience of print is just one more instance of the uptick in "sales of instant-film cameras, paper notebooks, board games and Broadway tickets"[2] that has made home brewing an antidote to Deliveroo and homeschooling the mirror image of TED Talks.

And yet, books are special—or at least have been treated as such, and are perhaps being treated as such more than ever. European laws continue to single out books: France's law against selling books below sticker price, for example, blocks supermarkets from competing with bookshops. The United States doesn't go that far, but our postal service does grant printed matter a special rate. And the judge who denied Kenneth Starr access to Kramerbooks' record of Monica Lewinsky's purchases believed that the books she'd gifted to President Clinton deserved greater privacy protection than did the matted poem she'd sent him on National Boss's Day or the sterling cigar holder that the *Starr Report* lists among the presents he gave her.[3]

Studying books can make it hard to venerate texts. I entered a doctoral program in comparative literature on the strength of teenage summers spent wishing that I could be a kinder Elizabeth Bennet or a more cheerful Jane Eyre. The first book history course I encountered, though, left me disappointed, dismayed, and finally depressed to learn that the publishing industry has never been propelled by great novels, poems, or plays. The 1,500 or so copies of *Pride and Prejudice* published in 1813 made no splash, but in the same year, poet laureate Robert Southey's biography of the scandalous navy hero Lord Nelson sold out twice, celebrity biographies being the closest thing to a sure bet in the most speculative of industries. Cookbooks fared even better.

Yet neither cookbooks nor biographies are what we talk about when we talk about The Book. For decades, the New York Public Library's wedding-ready lobby housed a case whose shatterproof glass might also conjure up thoughts of taxidermy. To call the double-columned, thousand-plus-page folio that the case protects from any human reader a Gutenberg Bible is to say that it's one of only 48 that survive of the approximately 180 Latin Bibles printed in Johannes Gutenberg's Mainz shop in the middle of the 1450s. The NYPL's copy was the first of those 48 to immigrate to America. On the wall next to the case, a plaque explains that upon the book's 1847 arrival at the New York docks, US Customs officials were asked to doff their hats. Copyright and tariff laws governing which books can enter the country bear an uncanny resemblance to immigration laws.[4] At the customs house, huddled masses of books can be quarantined or deported.[5] But the trophy collected by James Lenox, the third-richest man in New York, was welcomed by paparazzi.

The first Gutenberg to enter the New World, but hardly the last—for between Lenox's time and ours, Americans have been their most avid buyers. Auctions like the one at which Lenox snagged the Bible for £500 laundered new (and New World) wealth into old examples of movable type. Thanks to tools that weren't available in 1847, though, scholars have begun to question the nature and significance of those examples.

First, Americans' confidence that movable type had brought them a kind of modernity lacking from oral- or handwriting-based civilizations turned out to be based on a false premise. In 2001, high-resolution imaging and computational analysis brought two scholars, the bibliographer Paul Needham and the physicist Blaise Agüera y Arcas, to the startling conclusion that the type used to make this Bible wasn't, technically speaking, movable at all. When examined closely, each instance of a given letter looks slightly different. That variation suggests that sand rather than metal may have been the medium in which Gutenberg first cast type—which means in turn that the letters would have been too soft to be reused for multiple books. Metal was in fact first used a continent away: the oldest surviving book printed with metal movable type was written in Chinese by a Buddhist monk in Korea, where it was printed in 1377.[6] Gutenberg's monumental Bible, in contrast, may have pointed back to manuscript as much as forward to movable type.

More fundamentally, scholars have begun to question whether "print" means "great books." The earliest surviving specimen of printing in the West whose publication date we know for sure doesn't come from a grand Bible like the one in the NYPL lobby. It takes the form of one of the documents that Gutenberg and his partners churned out more frenetically than any book: papal indulgences.

In Manchester, a different rare-books library holds a sheet of vellum whose dimensions could lead you to mistake it, from a distance, for an 8 ½-by-11 photocopy. Its printed blanks are filled in with a handwritten inscription indicating the date on which it was sold—October 22, 1454—and the name of the woman who bought it, Margarethe Kremer. Indulgences raised money for timely causes by absolving purchasers like Kremer from their sins. (Her payment went to the defense of Cyprus against the Turks.) With their blank spaces meant to be filled in by sinful purchasers, they were the first form letters.

Indulgences aren't just one of the earliest productions of Gutenberg's press. They're also one of the most common. Besides Margarethe Kremer's, forty-nine copies of the same indulgence from 1454–1455 survive.[7] This may not sound like much, but it's double the number of Gutenberg Bibles printed during that time that have made it into the twenty-first century complete.

You might expect just the opposite. Physically, bound books are sturdier than loose leaves. And culturally, a large, expensive sacred volume (Gutenberg's Bibles weighed in at over a thousand pages and cost around a year of a master craftsman's salary) was likelier to be treasured and protected than a bureaucratic form.[8] Why, then, would twenty-first century libraries own more indulgences than Bibles?

The likeliest explanation is that indulgences were produced in very large numbers. A mass-produced object can survive despite a low preservation rate. This would become one of the advantages of printed books over manuscripts, which had been treasured precisely because they were rare and expensive. As printed books were to manuscript books, so Gutenberg's indulgences were to his Bibles. James Lenox bought immortality in the form of a marble library, but the case of the otherwise anonymous Margarethe Kremer shows that far flimsier purchases could bestow immortality too. Indulgences survive by accident: many copies whose blanks were not filled in have been preserved as binders' waste, recycled as raw material for the spines of later volumes.

Printed sheets sometimes preceded printed books. In fact, if you look closely at the Bibles that Gutenberg produced, they seem to ape the indulgences rolling off the same presses, even— by the time that type had become truly movable—recognizably reusing the same letters.[9] The blanks that his Bibles left for red letters and hand-decorated initial capitals may have been modeled on the fill-in-the-blank format of indulgences whose printed boilerplate was made to be completed by writing in the purchaser's name.[10]

In the seventeenth century, far from rendering manuscript obsolete, the easy availability of printing made handwriting more important than ever before, as printed forms (the descendants of those same indulgences) made it all the more crucial for middle-class people to know how to fill in the blanks.[11] Another result is that early printers saw books as a headache, indulgences as a godsend. Each indulgence was a single sheet on a single side, so there was no fiddling with the order of pages, and print runs were in the hundreds of thousands, so the start-up costs of setting type were quickly amortized. Furthermore, the fact that the church that commissioned them also bought the final product cut out the pesky distribution logistics required to sell books—not to mention the cut taken on book sales by carters, wholesalers, retailers, and everyone involved in supplying credit.[12]

Those indulgences remind us that from the very beginning, printing wasn't only or even primarily a tool for producing sacred texts or timeless literature. Just as not all books take the form of print (whether that's because they're gorgeously illuminated manuscripts or ruled Mead copybooks), conversely, not all print takes the form of books. In 1907, as bibliographer Simon Eliot points out, industry estimates put books at only 14 percent of the total value of print production in Britain. Printed literature formed an even smaller fraction, since the 14 percent included handwritten notebooks and account books. Measured by sheer number of pages that rolled off the press, there's never been a time when book-length volumes kept pace with "jobbing printing"—that is, single sheets paid in advance.

More than two centuries later, most printed paper is made to be thrown away. When David Mikics posits that "literature, music and art express; computers, by contrast, lead you in a step-by-step way," he might as well take Ikea assembly leaflets to prove that paper leads in a step-by-step way.[13] Ask someone to visualize a reader, and they're likeliest to picture a pair of hands holding a book. If you take durable, long-form texts as the paradigmatic printed matter, then much of what you read on-screen will indeed seem to fall short of that benchmark. Compare Facebook posts to Gutenberg's Bible, and civilization seems to be going down the drain. But compare tweets to indulgences, and it's much of a muchness.

Printers spent the centuries following Gutenberg diversifying into more secular genres: broadsides, handbills, tickets, bureaucratic forms, even food labels and betting slips. Examining the output of eighteenth-century America's most famous printer—Benjamin Franklin—James Green and Peter Stallybrass find auction announcements, handbills advertising rewards for runaway slaves, newspapers crammed with classified ads, and above all blank forms: lottery tickets, bills of lading, legal documents ("indentures" got their name from being torn jaggedly in half), and account books like the ones in which he himself recorded these transactions. According to an advertisement in the *Pennsylvania Gazette*, Ben Franklin's shop offered,

> Bills of Lading bound and unbound, Common Blank Bonds for Money, Bonds with Judgment, Counterbonds, Arbitration Bonds with Umpirage, Bail Bonds, Counterbonds to save Bail harmless, Bills of Sale, Powers of Attorney, Writs, Summons, Apprentices Indentures, Servants Indentures, Penal Bills,

Promissory Notes, &c all the Blanks in the most authentick
Forms, and correctly printed.

Printers in the American colonies depended even more than
their British counterparts on jobbing printing. The reason was
that luxury items, among which books counted, were cheaper
to import than to produce for a limited local audience. As a
result, Franklin also printed labels for medicine bottles, wrapping for soap, and "500 advertisements about thread."[14] What
he didn't print, with a handful of exceptions, was any object
that we would recognize today as a book—let alone as a work
of literature.

We think of the printed word as transcending space and
time, but jobbing printing was location based and date sensitive. Where defenders of print today accuse blogs and tweets of
destroying our power to immerse ourselves in the great classics,
Franklin's printing was already sound bite-sized, ephemeral,
and profit driven.

Even if you leave aside indulgences and classified ads, the
very books whose longevity we now use as a stick with which
to beat the obsolescence built into hardware and software was
in fact the first mass-produced consumer good to be marked
with its production date—and, whether by remaindering or by
recycling, an expiration date. When journalist Calvin Trillin
described the life span of a book as "somewhere between milk
and yogurt," he bracketed books with date-stamped perishables
rather than with treasured heirlooms.[15]

A looming sell-by date, in turn, may make renting more
attractive than owning. Polemics decrying "the end of ownership" often contrast electronic licensing with a printed past in

which buying a book meant that you could do whatever you wanted with it.[16] Here, too, rearview mirrors flatter. Young couples may choose to marry at the NYPL because bound and printed paper remains a marker of eternal commitments. But like staying married, sticking with a book for life may be intended more often than accomplished.

The first generation of commercial ebooks, print lovers soon discovered with dismay, couldn't be lent or even inalienably owned. Most of us, in fact, realized only long after pressing Amazon's "Buy" button that it should really have been labeled "Rent" or "License," for when you pay for the right to read an ebook, you're not buying the right to resell it or even to own it yourself forever. This may come as a surprise if you've never clicked through to Amazon's disclosure that "Kindle Content is licensed, not sold, to you by the Content Provider," and that "you may not sell, rent, lease, distribute, broadcast, sublicense, or otherwise assign any rights to the Kindle Content or any portion of it to any third party."[17]

Amazon's business model, in short, relies on its customers' failure to read the fine print (fine screen?). Scholar Keith Houston compares the ebook economy with a housing market in which readers, like "tenants, remain trapped on the wrong side of the divide."[18] But we should be careful not to blame on a technology what's in fact the result of a business model. Licensing restrictions don't inhere in screens any more than copyright law inheres in printed paper. Law, rather than technology, ensures that most commercially distributed ebooks today can be neither owned nor loaned. As manuscript, print, and electronic formats evolved, one thing that's never changed is that buying a book outright is the exception rather than the rule.

From the beginning, printed books were more often borrowed than owned. Moreover, much printed matter was bought by groups—a book club or, in the case of periodicals especially, a chain of readers who paid more or less depending on their place in the reading order. Newspapers were traditionally read first by a wealthy subscriber, then resold to a neighbor who paid a reduced price for yesterday's news, then passed down to below-stairs users—an unschooled seamstress who might use it to cut out patterns, or an illiterate cook who might use it to mop up spills.

Soon after the publication of *Mansfield Park*, Jane Austen complained that her readers were "more ready to borrow and praise, than to buy." They were borrowing at for-profit circulating libraries—most common in spa towns where vacationers had leisure to read—that doubled as venues for flirting, browsing, and occasionally talking about books. Where today's critics of digital licensing dismiss renting as a poor substitute for owning—assuming that the only party that it benefits is greedy corporations—middle-class Victorian readers paid a premium for the right to get rid of books after reading them. *David Copperfield*, *Jane Eyre*, *Middlemarch*—all the great realist novels were originally rented more often than bought. Their earliest readers saw them as disposable single-use items that you didn't want cluttering up your shelves once their brief life expectancy had elapsed, any more than you'd keep yesterday's newspaper. One 1845 journalist declared that "few are the works of fiction, as long and wearisome experience teaches, that you wish to select and purchase and place upon your shelves, as deserving of a second and a third perusal."[19] A year later, Balzac described a character who abandons his old mistress for a younger one, "without saying goodbye, as one throws away a novel after reading it."[20]

When Dickens's bookshelves were cataloged after his death, the absence of novels—except copies sent and signed by authors trying to cozy up to the great man—revealed how rarely fiction had made it onto his own shopping list. This is because most Victorian readers accessed fiction through a hybrid strategy: instead of choosing between borrowing and buying, readers followed one with the other. We can see this hybrid at work in the rules for one Yorkshire book club, pasted into the pages of an 1849 novel. In this club, each subscriber paid a guinea and a half to join and a guinea and a half each subsequent year (the equivalent of about $150 today). The rules stated that "no book be admitted which is either strictly professional, or on statistics, or the price of which shall exceed three guineas": one such book would have eaten up the profit of two whole memberships. Subscribers were allowed to borrow large books for ten days and small books for five days; distinctions among book sizes were often as sharp as the distinction between books and periodicals. The yellowing insert explicitly excludes Sundays from the day count; the library must have feared encouraging time-strapped members to cheat on the Sabbath.

Every December, the club's members met to auction off all of the books bought in the previous year, suggesting that they considered year-old books past their sell-by date—so much for the timelessness of print. Any books unlucky enough to find no takers were bought, like it or not, by the member who had originally ordered them. He or she (the subscribers included a few ladies) was required to pay half price and haul away the book, to leave space for newer volumes in the coming January.[21]

The assumption that books are made to be bought is in fact a recent innovation, propagated for commercial reasons by interested parties. In the nineteenth century, publishers began trying to persuade readers that far from showing generosity, sharing books was immoral or even disgusting. In 1855, the American magazine *Godey's Lady's Book* ran a story titled "The Life and Adventures of a Number of *Godey's Lady's Book* Addressed Particularly to Borrowers, Having Been Taken Down in Short-Hand from a Narration Made by Itself." The "number" (what we would call an issue) complains bitterly of the wear and tear that it suffered when lent by subscribers to all their friends. Each girl should buy her own copy, the long-suffering magazine declared, the same way she bought her own bonnet: "How would you like to have that passing from head to head?"

A cruder method was to reframe as theft what had long been understood as sociable sharing. In 1931, Bernays launched a contest "to look for a pejorative word for the book borrower, the wretch who raised hell with book sales and deprived authors of earned royalties." Entries included "book weevil," "borrocole," "libracide," "booklooter," "bookbum," "bookkibitzer," "culture vulture," "greeper," "bookbummer," "bookaneer," "blifter," "biblioacquisiac," "book buzzard," and "greader."[22]

In the new division of labor that Cold War publishers invented, hardbacks were for gifting and displaying, paperbacks for hiding and discarding.[23] Amazon's digital rights management (DRM) strategy made no provision for the gift giving of individual titles: you could buy a Kindle gift certificate, but particular ebooks needed to be bought—or rather licensed—by the end user.

Today, libraries continue to amortize the cost of each volume by spreading it over successive generations. Even readers who buy a printed book outright often do so in the expectation that they'll own it only temporarily. Resale value determines afford-ability: college students are willing to advance the price of that organic chemistry text because they trust that a few months later some unidentified stranger will take it off their hands.

Nothing more humbling than spotting the novel I assigned last semester back on my campus bookstore's shelves, especially when it's labeled "clean copy." But in an era of music and video streaming, owning a book may appear to students less like a sign of love than like economic wastefulness. The most recent studies of hard-copy textbooks suggest that 61 percent of students sold their textbooks at the end of the semester, while 51 percent just rent them in the first place. As a result, fewer than half of the students annotated their textbooks.[24]

The organization expert Marie Kondo prompted outrage in 2011 when she advised readers to throw away any book that fails to "spark joy"—including her own.[25] On the other hand, the workbook sold along with it proved a canny ploy to avoid undercutting her royalties with a flood of secondhand copies. When we think of the book as a cherished hand-me-down, we ignore how often, and how variously, they've been designed to be unloaded. Even as books have provided a guinea pig for commercial innovators from Gutenberg to Jeff Bezos, one constant has been their complicated relation to ownership. You can read a book without paying for it, thanks to organizations ranging from the Gideons to the public library system to the birdhouse-like structures known as Little Free Libraries. The Big Expensive Libraries maintained by state universities often make their hard-copy holdings available to all taxpayers but reserve for enrolled students their electronic subscriptions, at the behest of for-profit digital journal publishers.

Conversely, you can—and probably do—buy books without ever ending up reading them. Like an exercise bike rusting in the basement, a book gathering dust testifies to good intentions.[26] (I delay discarding books the same way my grandmother, who grew up during the Depression, waited for leftovers to rot in the fridge.) But a book sitting unread on the shelf is also like an unopened bottle of designer bubble bath. Just as Jacuzzis attract home buyers whose long hours at work preclude the self-indulgent soaks that they pictured while touring open houses, so a book makes its buyer feel guilty for not spending time where she has already spent money.[27]

Even when a book does remain in a reader's possession, that's no guarantee that it will absorb her from start to finish. In 2016, Amazon banned publishers putting the table of contents at the end of the book. Only once that prohibition hit the news did ordinary readers discover that the company's Kindle Unlimited subscription service had been paying publishers in proportion to the farthest page read—perversely, creating incentives to game the system by moving the most often-read content to the very end. On the face of it, nothing is more logical: a novel whose pages one turns convulsively until reaching the end should earn more than one whose readers drift away on page three. Yet by this measure, an encyclopedia whose users looked up a single entry on Xylography would look more thoroughly thumbed than one in which they'd consulted every single entry up through Woodcuts.

It's easy for teenagers who have never flipped through a printed user manual to associate books with losing oneself rather than with finding information. But given that both Bezos and his critics grew up with printed dictionaries, a likelier explanation for their blind spot lies in wishful thinking. The long dominance of books designed to be searched, skimmed, and discarded needs to be airbrushed out of our memories because it challenges the digital-age fantasy that print inculcates patience, strengthens work ethics, and stretches attention spans. "If you can incorporate the gym into your regular routine," the *New York Times* "Year of Living Better" lifehack column proclaims, "you can incorporate quality time with a book too."[28]

In 2013, David Mikics recommended "slow reading"—the verbal equivalent of making your own bread or knitting your own socks—as the ultimate digital detox. "If you're looking at this book," he told the readers of his acid-free hardcover volume, "you're committed"—to patience, to concentration, to deep thought. In choosing books over emails and tweets, "you have the chance to live up to that commitment." Digital pleasures, he seemed to be saying, were tempting weak-willed booklovers to betray a long-term relationship. Book reading became a retreat from digital chatter (as absolute as entering a monastery), a protest against consumer society (as bold as climbing the barricades), a therapy for racing brains and frenzied pulses.

A recent article in the *Guardian* complains, more specifically, that web browsing "fragments our attention span in a way that's not ideal if you want to read, for instance, *Clarissa*."[29] In one way, Samuel Richardson's great novel *Clarissa* is an obvious example to choose. Just under a million words in its first edition, the blow-by-blow story's winding verbiage led even Richardson's fan Samuel Johnson to declare that "if you were to read Richardson for the story, your impatience would be so much fretted that you would hang yourself." Paradoxically, though, that length prevented most readers from ever giving *Clarissa* their full attention. On first publication in 1748, the novel seems to have functioned more as background noise: in one 1756 diary, the historian Naomi Tadmor finds a cloth merchant reporting that "as I was writing all the even[ing] my wife read Clarissa Harlowe to me." When his human audiobook read aloud what he termed "the moving scene of the funeral of Miss: [*sic*] Clarissa Harlowe," the merchant continued to add up figures.[30] The absence of calculation errors testifies to the carefully titrated attention that he withheld from the story, as a driver today might keep one ear open to a podcast and another cocked for GPS directions.[31]

The merchant was unusual less in economizing the time and attention that he gave *Clarissa* than in leaving an articulate verbal trace of that experience. The irregular wear and tear that I found in library copies of novels like *Clarissa*—a heavily thumbed rape scene followed by pristine pages of landscape description, getting grimier again as the plot picked up— suggested that print readers who progress evenly from Page 1 to The End are as rare as rational economic actors.

The codex continued to tout its put-down-ability in the advertisements for one 1835 "Parlour-Table Book" whose publisher boasted that "it may be taken up and laid down without inconvenience." For us, interrupting a book denotes impulsivity and impatience. But for most of print's history, it proved civilized self-restraint. Where twentieth-century parents measured their children's impulse control by their ability to refrain from eating a marshmallow, earlier generations tested their resolve by the ability to refrain from racing through a book.[32]

For most of the half millennium since Gutenberg, readers have browsed and skipped their way around books: think (if you're old enough) of the walks that your fingers once took through the yellow pages. As evidence that we're not the first readers in history to complain of information overload, historian Ann Blair points to the notes taken by early modern scholars as well as to their printed equivalent, the then-mushrooming genre of the reference book. Fighting fire with fire, the scholars whose working methods Blair reconstructs responded to the glut of books with more books designed to summarize, abridge, or index the mass of printed matter that was too bulky to read from cover to cover.[33]

When one of the shrewdest analysts of digital reading, Clifford Lynch, called ebooks "more like reference databases than [like] traditional books that are read sequentially from beginning to end," he airbrushed out the long tradition of print that invites dipping and sampling—imposing our own order on the text, not submitting to its undertow.[34] When a British Library report lamented that academic researchers "go online to avoid reading in the traditional sense," the world's greatest research institution, too, ignored the long tradition of pick-and-choose reading.[35]

Nostalgists for print stack the deck by assuming a best-case scenario in which all printed books were great, and all reading rapt. Sven Birkerts, for example, complains that when his students open their laptops, "I pretend they are taking course-related notes, but would not be surprised to find out they are writing to friends, working on papers for other courses, or just trolling their favorite sites while they listen."[36] True enough— but the fact that a student's eyeballs were glued to a page has never been a guarantee that she was paying attention. As far back as thirteenth-century Russia, the Dutch paleographer

Erik Kwakkel finds a seven-year-old schoolboy decorating the margins of his birchbark class notes with a caricature.[37] Just over half a millennium later, as cheap wood-pulp paper replaced scarce rag-based predecessors, a new form of procrastination was born: the spitball. The laptop's real victim may not be the ability to pay attention so much as the skill of crafting an aerodynamic airplane from lined paper.[38]

When we think about the death of print, we're likelier to picture a rapt novel-reader than a ruled-notebook doodler. Pundits who compare the way we do use digital media with the way we wish we used printed books are often contrasting ideal apples with real oranges. Comparing the way people actually read print with the way they actually read electronic texts, on the other hand, would make it possible to either corroborate or contradict subjective perceptions.

Naomi Baron's ingenious strategy was to juxtapose surveys of college students' feelings about reading on paper and screen with experiments measuring the physiological effects of both.[39] Strangely enough, students' opinions ran directly counter to their behavior. Asked which medium they prefer, college students endorse print no less roundly than any middle-aged professor. (The exception, Baron notes wryly, is one student who complained, under the heading "Liked least about reading in hardcopy": "It takes me longer because I read more carefully.") Students in the United States, Germany, and even smartphone-dense Japan report that they understand and remember more on paper. Yet when tested for comprehension and retention, they score the same on paper as on-screen; nor do physiological measures of their eye movements show any difference between the two media. Even though subjects report more eyestrain with screens, the frequency with which they blink is identical for screen and paper.[40]

Trying to make sense of these contradictions, I find myself remembering the double-blind "violin experiment" carried out at the 2010 International Violin Competition of Indianapolis. Researchers challenged musicians to guess which of two instruments was a Stradivarius and which a violin a few days or weeks or years old. Blindfolded and asked to play two instruments doused with the same perfume, an overwhelming majority of participants identified the new violin as the one they'd like to take home with them—even though the very same musicians declared that they preferred older violins.[41] Here, too, nostalgia for an older technology makes self-reporting untrustworthy.

Baron hazards a more generous explanation. The experimental subjects were reading under lab conditions, on a schedule. When researchers lifted the time limits, in contrast, study participants consistently spent longer on print than on screens—and their comprehension varied accordingly.

But perhaps this is because around books, we expect more of ourselves. Imagine some study comparing the rate at which food gets chewed in a fast-food joint or in a fancy restaurant. The explanation wouldn't lie in the physical difference between plastic and silver forks. Printed books put us on our best behavior.

The irony is that books became talismans—empowered to silence cell phones or inculcate focus—in precisely the decade when historians were coming to agree that books have whatever powers their users vest in them. Adrian Johns's 1998 monograph *The Nature of the Book* showed how many centuries users of movable type took to make the assumptions about printed books that we make today: that every copy of the same edition can be treated as interchangeable, or that the place and date of publication listed in a book can be trusted. Where Cold War–era technological determinists like Elizabeth Einstein had argued that the material form of books mass-produced through movable type contributed to the Reformation and the Scientific Revolution, Johns asked instead how changing ideas, beliefs, and feelings shaped the use of books. Worrying that digital media will corrupt its users can lead us to cast books as omnipotent—their presence magically guarantees virtue, their absence vice. But Johns suggests that human beings can alter the book's function just as dramatically as books change their users.

I described early printed books as standardized, but it might be more accurate to say that they were *perceived* as standardized. To our eyes today, early books look more like fraternal than identical twins. Different copies of the same edition were customized with different bindings. More importantly, those copies might even have contained subtly different texts, thanks to so-called stop-press corrections made when an error was caught as the first sheets rolled off the press.

Only centuries later could the owner of one copy of a particular edition of a particular text feel confident that distant owners of other copies were holding a functionally interchangeable object in their hands. Even then, Johns shows that confidence to be the product of social conventions, not just technological possibilities. "Functionally" is key because one of those social conventions was the unstated agreement to ignore differences in binding and size and paper, to assume that for all intents and purposes these different objects were the same.

The perception of standardization also made possible citation as we know it. In footnoting a page number for the book that I just referenced, I'm wagering that the copy you pull down from your shelf or your server will be identical to the book lying on the desk in front of me. We distinguish digitizations of printed books from "born-digital" books, whose texts went straight from a word processor to an ebook file. The metaphor obscures the fact that pbooks and ebooks alike are made, not born.[42]

———

In 2015, faced with complaints of headaches and eyestrain, Google issued a disclaimer that its wearable Glass was not "designed for . . . reading 'War and Peace.'"[43] "Things like that are better done on bigger screens," the spokesperson added drily. Media scholar Clay Shirky points out that that same novel happens to be the only literary work mentioned by name in Carr's article "Is Google Making Us Stupid?"[44] (Carr had exemplified internet-induced dumbness by quoting a doctor's confession of losing patience with Tolstoy's masterpiece.) And Michael Harris's 2014 meditation *The End of Absence* recommends reading *War and Peace*, a book that's "thirteen hundred (long) pages long and weighs the same as a dead cat," as a way to distract oneself from the buzzing of the cell phone.[45] The devil makes work for idle fingers.

When Carr adds that "a book, if it is going to be a true book, needs to be more than a container of words; it needs to be a shield against busyness, a transport to elsewhere,"[46] the tacked-on qualifier "if it is going to be a true book" makes clear that not all books fit that lofty bill. The yellow pages don't still users' thumbs; neither do podcasted short stories or tweeted poems. Often, booklovers are thinking of a subset of books defined by a medium but also by a particular scale and a particular genre, one they assume to be read in a particular way. Call it Long-form Literary Print.

We fetishize books because we imagine that they can protect us from our distractibility, our sloth, the weakness of will that the earliest monks called acedia.[47] Long before clickbait, reading was already entangled with worries about who was in control: the reader or the text. The very term "page-turner" attributes to books a mind of their own. The momentum of the gathered and bound pages appears to drag a helpless reader in its wake, as if every book were one of those rare volumes whose pages flip mechanically inside a glass case displayed in a library lobby.[48]

Eighteenth-century readers worried just as much as their twenty-first-century counterparts about pace or completeness—but they worried in the opposite direction, stigmatizing lazy, passive readers who allowed inertia to drag them along from start to finish. As literary critic Nicholas Dames explains, "The media it is now seen as a bulwark against—film, television, electronic technology—are described in precisely the same terms as an earlier tradition had explained the novel itself."[49] Just over a century ago, one moralist warned that "some people cannot stand very exciting or thrilling stories, just as some people are better without any wine." Readers were advised to swear off novels, "unless, indeed, you can train yourself to sufficient self-control resolutely to keep their fascination under mental lock and key—a grand piece of self-discipline in itself."[50] Today, we outsource our willpower to print.

Like digital reading, print reading has been shaped by the tension between centripetal and centrifugal impulses, between readers' desire to disassemble books and reshuffle or reassemble them with others, and readers' desire to cocoon themselves within the covers of a single book, to use the finitude of the book to block out the paralyzing range of possibilities offered by a library. Reading on digital devices where books must compete not just with other books but with shorter and more visually arresting media—for the printed book, unlike its manuscript forbears, makes its black-and-white form deliberately dowdy—throws into relief the printed book's power to focus its readers.

Even a defender of digital media like Steven Johnson can call print books "a kind of game preserve for the endangered species of linear, deep-focused reading."[51] British novelist Will Self warned in 2014 that if soon "the vast majority of text will be read in digital form on devices linked to the web," the fate of the novel depends on whether "readers will voluntarily choose to disable [internet] connectivity." If they won't, Self predicts, long fiction can't compete.[52]

A digital device offers an infinity of activities among which any particular text can get lost. In contrast, as science writer Annie Paul observes, "the built-in limits of the printed page are uniquely conducive to the deep reading experience."[53] Essayist Michael Harris reflects, similarly, that "book-oriented styles of reading opened the world to me—by closing it."[54]

The blindfolding exercise my students attempt each year focuses them by eliminating the distraction of the words on the page. So, too, the printed book's unique selling point is turning out to be its limits: the choices that it refuses to present, the infinity of mental paths that its closed form bars us from taking.

Like horses, readers need blinders. We enlist print in what the political philosopher Jon Elster calls a Ulyssean contract. Just as Odysseus binds himself to the mast because he doesn't trust his future self not to leap overboard in pursuit of sirens, so I board a Wi-Fi-free plane carrying only a Penguin Classic that I've spent years trying and failing to finish. When in 2017 a xenophobic administration banned laptops on flights entering the United States from ten airports in majority-Muslim countries, I found myself, for the first time in a decade, reading a novel in one transatlantic sitting.

The same hucksters who once peddled get-literate-quick speed-reading techniques now advertise "zenware" (Freedom, LeechBlock, Chrome Nanny) to block us from racing through, and around, our online reading. Yet the strongest ropes may remain Gutenberg's. "Nuns fret not at their convent's narrow room," Wordsworth wrote in a sonnet meditating on the freedom that fixed poetic forms confer. ("Stanza" is Italian for both a section of a poem and a room in a building.) As poets have sometimes welcomed formal constraints, so digital-age readers are learning to cultivate material limits. In choosing to read in print rather than online, one's present self can choose to quarantine the pop-up windows and online games that one's future self might otherwise choose. The first ebook bestseller, *Fifty Shades of Grey,* dramatized an English major's craving for constraint. Readers now boast, rather than confess, to being held spellbound.

One blustery February afternoon, the class that had played Name That Book took a field trip. A school bus whose bright yellow looked like something out of a Richard Scarry illustration ferried us to an exurb an hour west of Boston, where a climate-controlled Home Depot–style hangar refrigerates Harvard Library's 10 million least-loved volumes in off-site storage. A clang drew our gaze upward: twenty men were shoveling snow from three acres of roofs. Beyond the fumes of the loading dock, neither leather spines nor wood shelving lay in sight. Instead, my students encountered fluorescent lights, linoleum floors, metal carts, plastic bins sold by the thousand-count, an eyewash, and a stenciled hard-hat reminder. Climbing on the cherry picker for a high-tech hayride, the students looked about as credible as politicians posing in a tank.

Stored at a temperature inhospitable to human bodies, the books in Harvard's depository also inhabit a scale incomprehensible to human minds. As tall as five people stacked on top of one another, the sublime crags of the depository's thirty-foot-high metal shelves produce the same vertigo as a stark cliff face.[55] On campus, books are shelved by subject; here, by height. Arriving at the depository, each volume encounters a sizing tray reminiscent of the devices into which you cram your hand luggage at the airport to test whether it will fit into the overhead bin. Also on arrival at the depository, each book's title is replaced with a bar code readable by a pistol-grip Motorola scanner: prisoner without a name, cell without a call number.

The ticket to this Siberia isn't always one-way. At some point in their exile, the luckiest books will be released at the request of a catalog user. If that user requests hard copy, the volume will be zapped by a scanner in the grippy-gloved hands of a fluorescent-lumbar-support-clad worker riding a cherry picker, bundled into a plastic bin, shunted onto a metal hand-truck, and loaded into an eighteen-wheeler to trundle past the sentry box and the nearby Kwik Print to the highway leading to campus, and finally into the reader's hands. When books do make the trip down the highway that our school bus took, they travel—as Jeffrey Schnapp's vivid documentary about the depository points out—11 million times slower than a packet of digital information. More often, therefore, the catalog user requests page images—meaning that the lucky volume will be scanned without ever escaping the building.

No sooner did Harvard's library announce that infrequently consulted journals would be evicted to the depository than impromptu civil disobedience campaigns arose, readers manically requesting entire runs of periodicals whose pages they never had time to open. Putting down a book seemed as cruel as putting down a pet dog. (In contrast, only a few student picketers protested when the college's most popular course, Introduction to Computer Science, commandeered the on-campus library's main reading room to hold office hours.)

Yet, difficult as it is for us to imagine a post-paper world, classical civilizations managed just fine without it. Clay or wax tablets, stone, papyrus, parchment: all of these seemed adequate to write on until a material that miraculously combined durability with portability and affordability came along. Stone lasts but can't be carried; papyrus is light but brittle and vulnerable to climate; parchment is as expensive as the animals that are skinned to make it. Outside of cemeteries and law offices, paper shunted many of those surfaces aside. Odds are that you are not reading this book on a clay tablet, a coconut husk, a palm leaf, or a piece of parchment, papyrus, or even a sheet of paper recycled from linen rags.

Invented in China around the beginning of the Common Era and brought to Europe via Muslim Spain just over a mil-

lennium later, paper soon generated as much buzz as any e-ink
technology today. The newfangled material offered a fourth ben-
efit on top of price, weight, and longevity: where papyrus and
parchment could be scraped clean and reused, paper's absorption of ink made it unerasable. The disadvantage of being less
recyclable was outweighed by the advantage of being less vulnerable to forgery. Our Etch A Sketch–like e-readers may bear
more resemblance to paper's predecessors than to the medium
invoked by the name of Amazon's Paperwhite e-reader.

Like e-readers, paper aroused controversy. What pro-
vokes nostalgia today was once seen as an enemy to tradition:
thirteenth-century sheep and cattle breeders had lobbied for a
papal decree invalidating documents on paper. That it offered
a cut-rate substitute for parchment doesn't mean that paper
wasn't expensive in absolute terms: though one Bible no longer
required herds of sheep to be slaughtered, until two centuries
ago paper remained the single biggest cost in most book production. Our now-dying custom of starting a business letter
halfway down the page comes from a time when wasting an
expensive sheet marked respect, the epistolary equivalent of a
potlatch.

One factor driving up prices was the raw materials: where
Asian paper incorporated mulberry bark, Europeans made it
from linen rags. In England, the expense of old clothes was
compounded by paper taxes, which served both to finance wars
and to limit the circulation of news. What open source and
Creative Commons are today, campaigns against "taxes on
knowledge" were for Victorian radicals who understood taxes
on paper and postage as an indirect form of censorship. Only
in the second half of the nineteenth century did the lifting of

those duties combine with steam technology and plant-based raw materials to make paper cheap enough to be disposable. As paper bags and toilet paper came onto the market, old newspapers were suddenly redundant.

Even today, in the age of scans and bar codes, we haven't really disowned paper. Essayist Ian Sansom points out that even travelers who check in with an electronic ticket still vomit into a paper bag and repair the damage with a wet wipe (invented in 1915). One could add that even the two months of the year when e-readers, hardbacks, and paperbacks sell most briskly are kicked off with a paper shredder; after New York's 2012 Thanksgiving parade, spectators piecing together confetti discovered that they were recycled from confidential police records.[56] It remains to be seen whether books will have more in common with playing cards and money—paper goods for which digital equivalents quickly emerged—or with tea bags and diapers.

A recent toilet-paper ad showed a tech-savvy man scolding his wife for scribbling on scraps of old-fashioned paper; when he shouts out from the toilet that there's nothing left on the cardboard roll, she slips under the door his paper-thin iPad.[57] The bathroom, this play on paperlessness reminds us, may be the last reading room whose contents will never be shipped to the depository.

Chapter 3

READING ON THE MOVE

I N THE MIDST of the 2013 Supreme Court hearings on the Defense of Marriage Act, which sought to outlaw same-sex unions, Amazon aired an advertisement for its newest e-reading device. Side by side on lounge chairs against a backdrop of beach umbrellas, a man strikes up a conversation with his bikini-clad neighbor: "That's a Kindle, right?"

She looks up from her reading. "Yeah, it's the new Kindle Paperwhite," she replies.

"I love to read at the beach," the man says. "But . . ."

"This is perfect at the beach," the woman reassures him. "And with the built-in light, I can read anywhere, anytime."

After a pause spent squinting down at his iPad again, the man announces triumphantly, "Done!"

"With your book?" asks the straight woman—literally straight, as we're about to discover. For when the man explains that, on the contrary, he's done buying a new Kindle device and invites his neighbor to celebrate, she sidesteps the question by noting demurely that her husband is bringing her a drink. Her comment sets up the Kindle buyer's newly topical punchline: "So is mine."

The Kindle ad equates modernity with mobility: the freedom to marry who you want with the freedom to read wherever you want. Expanding on the theme two years later, Amazon marketers began to solicit photos with the hashtag #haveKINDLEwill TRAVEL. The resulting flood of images—a white man holds a Kindle on a dirt road; a white man reads silhouetted against a bell tower; a pair of white palms cradle a Kindle in a windowsill overlooking a cliff—measure the power of the device by the sublimity of the landscapes that it blots out.[1] (Only the most riveting read can compete with the Taj Mahal.) Borrowing Microsoft's metaphor of the "window," Amazon's al fresco scenes naturalized an otherwise daunting new technology. The wage slave might hunch over a computer in a fluorescent-lit cubicle, but the Kindle's user remained a free spirit, shaded by trees that memorialized now-obsolete wood-pulp paper.[2]

Yet Amazon's 2013 ad's celebration of the latest legal decision turns out to look oddly atavistic. Amazon's his-'n'-hers contrast harks back to a paperback-era *New Yorker* cartoon where the symmetry of identical bedside reading lamps belies the contrast between a woman's book and her husband's antennae peeking out from behind his newspaper.

And even that pun on twentieth-century bestseller *Men Are from Mars, Women Are from Venus* can be traced in turn to the nineteenth-century iconography that associated men with the ephemeral, fragmentary, fast-moving modernity of the newspaper. In contrast, the heroine of one Victorian novel hesitates even to touch a newspaper, managing instead to pinch it "delicately between her finger and thumb; for the Carlingford papers were inky and badly printed, and soiled a lady's hand."[3]

Kindle is to book as iPad is to newspaper: one self-contained (designed for offline reading of durable long-form text), the other outward pointing (designed for online browsing of constantly refreshed snippets). Whether men are shown with paper broadsheets or with electronic tablets, cartoonists continue to picture women clinging to the always-about-to-be-superseded book.

Those cartoonists have a point, for industry statistics cast what looks like a reading gap as something more specific: a book-reading gap. In most parts of the world, including the United States, books remain the province of white women, while magazines and newspapers come closer to being evenly distributed. Even as Amazon's ad celebrates the freedom to marry whomever we like, its ad still counts on the viewer to place reading habits on a gender binary.

But this gender gap might be less about men's and women's device preferences than about the time they have to devote to reading in any medium. In an 1869 etiquette manual, the Anglican moralist Charlotte Yonge explained why women read more than men: "There are so many hours of a girl's life when she must sit still," according to Yonge, "that a book is her natural resource."[4] Most American parents today would nod in recognition at Yonge's claim that girls read more. That may be because reading thrives on the absence of opportunity cost. Books find readers when more lucrative work is ruled out by gender (earning eighty-three cents on the dollar, American women outspend on books) as well as age (literature reading is highest among those too young or old for paid employment).

Once a sign of economic power, reading has become the province of those whose time lacks value.

Yonge's observation would have startled her grandparents, though. For most of British history, men across all social classes read more and read better than women. Only in the nineteenth century did women's literacy begin to climb faster than men's, finally overtaking it at century's end.[5] Today in developing countries, girls' literacy continues to lag.[6] Economically, that makes perfect sense. Investment in boys' education promises payoff in the form of high wages, while teaching girls to read withdraws their short-term unpaid work from the household.

Only thanks to servants was the time that Yonge's readers spent outside of the labor force freed up for reading. As a new parent condemned Tantalus-like to push a stroller through the library without stopping anywhere except story hour, I, too, began to wish that bookstores would sell babysitting coupons. Unopened novels found themselves crushed by a stack of the board books that I read with near-liturgical regularity, *Goodnight Moon* replacing bedtime prayers. In the small fraction of brain not devoted to memorizing Dr. Seuss, I remembered Schopenhauer's joke: "It would be a good thing to buy books if one could also buy the time in which to read them."[7]

The defenders of print books are as likely to forget this as the sellers of e-readers. The volunteers of Britain's Reading Agency could usefully remember Schopenhauer's aphorism as they plan this year's celebration of the annual World Book Night. A few years ago, I accompanied an alumna of the course where we played Name That Book as she marked Shakespeare's birthday by handing out free copies of a movie tie-in paperback,

The Perks of Being a Wallflower, on the Boston T. She had been instructed to give copies to "infrequent readers"—but how to profile the hurrying commuters by their likelihood of already having reading material in their backpacks? In the sea of faces reflected in glowing smartphones or canted toward billboards, it proved hard to spot a reader for whom a giveaway wouldn't prove redundant.

At a historical moment when paperbacks litter curbs and ebooks can be downloaded for free by the thousands, the obstacle to reading isn't getting your hands on a book; it's finding time to read it. The volunteers who celebrate World Book Night by handing out paperbacks might be confusing objects with practices—things with experiences. Yet media history reveals that what gets people to read, or stops them from doing so, is rarely the presence or absence of just the right gadget.

Marketing campaigns that tout the portability of e-readers recycle an older triumphalist history that depicted monumental, site-specific volumes giving way to handier, nimbler printed pamphlets, books, and periodicals. Ever since the beginning of the print era, the reformers who made books' mobility stand for readers' modernity cast this change as not only an inevitability but an improvement: more freedom, less friction. Erica Jong might have called it a zipless read.

In reality, sedentary books were never really swept aside by nomadic successors. Already in the late Middle Ages, hefty volumes chained in hulking cathedrals coexisted happily with "girdle books" hung from clothing—the earliest wearables. Oxford University Press's 1875 India-paper Bible used the new technology of onionskin pages to slim down its contents as elegantly as any MacBook Air, without ever throwing lectern-sized Bibles out of work.

How big your reading matter is turns out to hinge more on where it's consumed than on when. Amazon's fantasy of books without borders airbrushed out the commercial strategies that made e-reading more site specific than print had ever been. Not only do the ebooks available depend on what copyright area you inhabit, but the device on which you encounter those books is determined largely by where you live. Next to income, the best predictor of whether you read on a large or small screen is nationality.[8] Throughout East Asia, phone reading caught on before dedicated e-readers had a chance to break in on their market. French ebooks gravitate to laptops, while book-length content is likelier to be found on Americans' tablets. In Britain, e-readers have begun losing ground to phones.[9] How a nation reads turns out to be as distinctive as what: even when the same *texts* circulate across the anglophone world, they take the form, once again, of different *books*. Yet the implicit claim of Amazon's ad campaigns that reading is getting better every day in every way emerged long before electronic media did.

Back in New York Public Library's lobby, I crane my neck to take in a four-part mural that wraps around the foyer like two ripped-apart page spreads. The first panel poses a larger-than-life Moses with the Tablets of the Law. Both elbows braced, five fingers splay and another five clench to support the weight of a supersized hunk of stone. This version of a handheld tablet bears five of the Ten Commandments, though an inadvertent scrambling of two Hebrew letters has turned "thou shalt not steal" into "thou shalt not wipe." The remaining five are relegated to a heap of shards at Moses' feet. Their jagged disarray reminds viewers that stone, however monumental, lacks the tensile strength that allows paper's cellulose web to bend without breaking.[10]

Moses's tablets dwarf the printed sign explaining that the mural was commissioned from Edward Laning in 1938 by Roosevelt's Works Progress Administration, that attempt to revive for a secular age the publicly accessible art that once lived in medieval cathedrals. Three more panels complete Laning's narrative. On the next wall, a monk hunches over a lectern, his shoulders and wrists as tightly rolled as his manuscript. At his feet, a book's clasps seal it as hermetically as the cloister encloses the monk.

Laning's third panel leads us back outdoors to the fifteenth-century German marketplace where a bearded Gutenberg, aided by a burly pressman, shows the local political boss his double-columned proof sheet for the first Bible ever printed. From Palestine to Germany, then westward again: the final panel lands us here in New York, where a fin de siècle gas lamp reveals the besuited owner of the *New York Tribune*, Whitelaw Reid, and the inventor Otthmar Mergenthaler eyeing a sheet printed by Linotype, the method of casting an entire line of type at once that displaced letter-by-letter typesetting in newspapers well into my own lifetime. In the background, a young news vendor shouts out the headlines. The only female figure whom Laning includes is smaller, above one door. There, a mother teaches her son to read. When the goal is a literate new generation of men, women's literacy is only important as a means to an end.

Laning called his series *The Story of the Recorded Word*. Taken together, though, the four panels tell stories, plural. As you circle the lobby en route to the printed paper you're after (or manuscripts, microfilms, or digital catalog records), you progress not just from past to present and East to West, but also from stone to wood pulp. That means from sacred to commercial, from monumental to portable, from precious to universally available, and from the timelessness of the Decalogue to the timeliness of tomorrow's fish-'n'-chips paper.

The grandeur of Laning's Art Deco murals risks overshadowing the 125 miles of stacks that, Atlas-like, hold up the football-field-sized reading room. The content of Laning's images, though, undercuts his chosen medium—the mural—by emphasizing the advantages of flimsy, nondescript paper. Precisely because of its expense, stone has usually been the medium of choice for one-offs—tombstones, for example. In contrast, parchment and, even more, paper lend themselves to multiple copies, decoupling the survival of the text from the durability of any one of its instantiations.

Paradoxically enough, expense also exposes stone to destruction: reuse value makes those tombstones worth rubbing out and re-chiseling, where the cheap modern rag paper shown in panel four isn't worth the trouble of erasing. Laning wanted to emphasize the dignity of the leather-aproned worker who shares the frame with his boss. Yet he draws just as much attention to the muscled man's inanimate counterparts—to the humble but hardworking wood pulp and self-effacing mass-produced print that crowd out the more glamorous, ceremonial, richly textured media such as stone and parchment.

As Laning's panels juxtapose sacred with commercial writing, they also contrast indoor spaces with outdoor ones. A circuit of the room takes viewers from a lightning-bathed mountaintop, to a day-lit scriptorium, to a newsroom's lamplight, only to end up back outside again with the bareheaded youth whom Laning painted above the Salomon Reading Room door. Stretched under a tree with Huck Finn–like abandon, he's tossed his hat onto the grass. Unlike the customs officials at the New York docks, he's not doffing to the Gutenberg Bible across the lobby. Unlike the inhabitants of the next-door Rose Main Reading Room, he doesn't rest his hardback on a table or his own back on a chair. Instead of a painted ceiling, he sits beneath a tree uncannily like the oak whose branches crown Amazon's Kindle icon almost a century later. Lolling on the grass without worrying about stained pages, this reader makes books al fresco as characteristically modern, and American, as the picnic.

Or, perhaps, as the bookmobile. Walk past Laning's panels into the wood-pulp-filled, wood-paneled reading room, and you can request a 1901 pamphlet in which the American librarian Melvil Dewey (better known for his eponymous decimal system) declares the new century an age of "traveling libraries." By this, he didn't mean bookmobiles. His goal was, instead, to build a collection that would rotate through rural branch libraries, themselves stationary but constantly unburdening and restocking their shelves with new deliveries. This analog "refresh" button would periodically update the titles available to local users.

Dewey freighted such "itinerating libraries" with more than practical importance. In the new century and the New World, he boasted, "the cheapness and quickness of modern methods of communication" makes books "grow wings." As smugly as any i-marketer, Dewey bragged that texts "which were thought to belong like trees in one place may travel about like birds."[11] The grand staircases leading up to Andrew Carnegie's free public libraries associate books quite literally with upward mobility—just as Carnegie's own life story credited rising with reading. Dewey attributed that uplift more specifically to deracinated books, as if social mobility depended on the material movement of paper.

The new American century made books pioneers. Calling "the traveling book" "the precursor of the traveling library," Dewey contrasted a bookmobile-filled America with a dark European past in which readers had to walk "hundreds of miles, perhaps begging their way, to read some book securely chained to a pillar."[12] The chains meant to protect books from theft appear here more like a means of imprisoning them. Where once readers traveled to books, now books would seek out their readers: adventurous volumes playing Odysseus to passive human Penelopes.

Dewey's allusion to mendicant friars invokes a Protestant gothic that recasts each new technology as another dissolution of the monasteries. I once was bound but now am free: as the text's power to liberate minds becomes the book's to shake off its chains, the Prometheus of Laning's grand ceiling changes from a reader to an object being read. The artist's confusion of books with readers prefigures the anthropomorphism of visionary Stewart Brand's 1985 claim that "information wants to be free."[13]

Brand's want was Dewey's need. "Libraries must be mobilized," the library reformer wrote; "books must travel." Nothing worse than staying on the shelf. Walter Benjamin would later compare buying "a book abandoned on the market place" with "the way the prince bought a beautiful slave girl in 'The Arabian Nights.'"[14] As Benjamin's collector manumits an individual book, so Dewey saw himself as emancipating an entire medium.

That portable books were associated with freedom didn't mean that the wares themselves were free. London publisher Allen Lane sold the first English paperbacks on train platforms, branching out in 1937 to vending machines with the start-up-esque name "Penguincubators." The perfect fit for a uniform-pocket sized for an entrenching tool, Lane's invention took off thanks to World War II. (Ironically, their standardized size and color coding by subject imitated the softcovers already being published by the Albatross Press in Hamburg.[15]) Long before ebooks, the cheap softcover reprint allowed the field to displace the library. Eventually, like so many other military technologies that subside to civilian uses, Lane's brainchild would allow books to flee the desk for the bus and the treadmill.

In 1958, an expert predicted that microfilms would replace books only once "some genius develops a way for reading them everywhere that books can be read: in the subway, in the bathtub, in a fishing skiff."[16] In practice, of course, a fishing skiff had never been the easiest place to read an exhibition catalog or a folio dictionary. That those were not the examples to which microfilm was expected to live up suggests that by 1958, Lane had succeeded in making the "book" synonymous with the paperback. Light enough to be carried, flexible enough to be pocketed, and cheap enough to be replaced if the hypothetical skiff capsized, his life-jacket-hued Penguins made bed, bath, and beyond the frontiers that every subsequent reading technology—should its sellers hope to earn a profit—would be challenged to conquer.

In the process, watertightness became a symbol of user-friendliness. In the early years when e-readers still commanded enough of a market to be worth fighting over, Kobo's release of a waterproof e-reader goaded Amazon to hire product testers to spray Kindles with saline solution.[17] The ebook rebranded itself as a u-book: *u* for "underwater," *u* for "ubiquitous."[18] Marketed by contradistinction to the desktop computers that replaced chained folios, the off-road device vended by Amazon and its beleaguered competitors might more precisely be termed the "e-paperback."

But perhaps the real reading revolution has had less to do with where liberated customers read books than where savvy marketers sold them. The novelty of paperbacks didn't just lie in the physical lightness of their covers, but also with the social insight that newspapers weren't the only printed commodity that could be funneled through "drug-stores, variety stores, stationery stores, cigar stores, confectionery stores, super-markets, railway stations, airports."[19] Tempting readers daily rather than during the occasional pilgrimage to a bookstore, Lane brought the mountain to Mohammed.

Where Ben Franklin's printshop sold chocolate and snuff, conversely Penguin funneled paperbacks to tobacconists. Amazon's pseudotelepathic Whispernet promised that "you can be anywhere in Sprint's high-speed data network coverage area, think of a book, and get it in one minute."[20] Later, in-app purchases promised even more instant gratification. Jeff Bezos was copying Lane's realization that mobile reading implied ubiquitous buying.

Amazon isn't the only tech company that's discovered that trick. Google Books founded its 25-million-volume digitization project not in the otherwise canonical garage, but in Oxford University's library stacks, where, as the company itself tells the story, Google employees watched "the librarians bring out centuries-old 'uncut' books that have only rarely seen the light of day."[21] Historian Anthony Grafton calls this the "sleeping beauty" trope: the book slumbering until the right reader kisses it awake.[22] As darkness equates stacks with dungeons, Dewey's contrast between roots and wings gives way to a vertical split between the basement and the cloud.

Libraries have been variously treated as living rooms, labs, playgrounds, and battlefields. But the very commercial giants that mine them for raw materials also cast them as dungeons from which books need to be sprung. Whether vehicled by steam railways or by fiber-optic cable, the logistical freedom afforded by books that can be read anywhere—more: bought anywhere—symbolizes the escape that imaginative literature is tasked with brokering. Yet Google's claim to liberate imprisoned libraries also casts a public-spirited veneer over its sale of book readers' attention to advertisers. Tech companies' promises of texts that can be read anywhere and anytime, meanwhile, follow Allen Lane in confusing readers' access to ideas with publishers' access to customers.[23]

None of this is to deny that reading has changed over time. (Book historians like me, after all, spend our working lives studying those changes.) But its evolution turns out to be explained just as much by the development of new technologies as by the emergence of new settings for reading. In the eighteenth century, when a new cult of nature encouraged hikers to cram poetry anthologies into their rucksacks, Rousseau set the fashion for traversing a page at the same time as a mountain. Books kept on moving at a pedestrian pace until, half a century later, engineer John McAdam's eponymous "macadam," which smoothed roads by covering soil with a layer of crushed, single-sized stones, decoupled reading from vomiting. As long as seats with minimal suspension bumped along uneven stone surfaces, squinting over a swaying book had few charms: in the seventeenth century, diarist Samuel Pepys testified that it was more comfortable to sing rounds with the strangers he met on the coach.[24] Only a multitasker as efficient as Napoleon could devour bestsellers nonstop in his carriage, tossing finished volumes out of the window as we might throw out a used Coke can.[25] The eccentricity of this practice can be measured by the fact that Thackeray expected readers to get the joke in the first chapter of his novel *Vanity Fair*, where the short, half-French upstart Becky Sharp flings a copy of Johnson's Dictionary out of a moving carriage.

Laning divided his panels in the New York Public Library according to the changing technologies through which texts get made. But book sizes were determined as much by the changing environments that books inhabited. As candles gave way to gas, then gas to electricity, portable lighting enabled reading to colonize the margins of the workday: the bedside novel, the newspaper skimmed en route to work. Commuters wedged in between books, reading sandwiched between scheduled activities: by 1855 the economist Walter Bagehot observed train passengers "tak[ing] their literature in morsels, as they take sandwiches on a journey."[26] As heavy tomes went the way of sit-down dinners, reading oozed into the dead zones of delays, transit, in-betweenness. In the process of worming their way into ever more venues, books also colonized ever more nooks and crannies of time.

More fundamentally, new physical settings empowered print to referee social relationships. First, horse-drawn omnibuses made it possible to read fellow commuters' books as easily as one's own. Eyeing the first installment of Dickens's *Little Dorrit* over the shoulder of a passenger on a Manchester bus in 1855, Elizabeth Gaskell complained that her fellow traveler "was such a slow reader ... you'll sympathize.... [with] my impatience at his never getting to the bottom of the page."[27] Next, in railway carriages so new that their etiquette remained to be established, spread-eagled broadsheets introduced strangers to one another. "Always Be Polite When Traveling," warned a cartoon that showed a gambler offering to share the sports page of his newspaper with the clergyman buried in a stouter, squatter tome on the opposite site of his train compartment.[28]

The same objects that tempted Gaskell to snoop and helped the fictional gambler break conversational ice, however, could work on the contrary to screen readers from each other, providing an excuse to ignore others who were physically present. One 1857 etiquette expert warned that while "civilities should be politely acknowledged" on public transport, "a book is the safest resource for an 'unprotected female.'"[29] Travelers privatized public transportation by retreating into the fold of a page as snails shrink into their shells. As new kinds of vehicles forced strangers together, print became their chaperone. Kafka called books an axe to break the frozen sea within their reader. But the book can also be a defensive weapon.

Outside of public transit, books filled more painful waits. A few hours into labor, about to give birth to the future author of *Frankenstein* at the cost of her own life, Mary Wollstonecraft scribbled a note to her husband, William Godwin: "Pray send me the newspaper. I wish I had a novel or some book of sheer amusement to excite curiosity and while away the time. Have you anything of the kind?"[30] Caregivers, too, need distraction, as Queen Victoria's future prime minister William Gladstone realized when he stationed himself outside of his terminally ill father's bedroom with a dimly lit volume of Henry Mayhew's protosociological treatise *London Labour and the London Poor.*[31] Reading carves out the space in which we wait for a baby to be born or a parent to die. Fear of death needs beguiling in more public spaces too. Fifty-two libraries opened in the London Underground when it was used for bomb shelter during the 1940–1941 Blitz.[32]

On the battlefield, too, reading has numbed physical and emotional pain. As I type with my right fingers, my left palm cradles a smartphone-sized 1836 reprint of American lexicographer Lyman Cobb's *The Reticule and Pocket Companion; or, Miniature Lexicon of the English Language.* The same dictionary whose folio edition holds ponderous audiences on a library lectern can go off-road in a man's pocket or a woman's protopurse "reticule." We know what paths this book traveled, because a date (June 4, 1863) is palely inked next to its owner's name and the name of the Union army unit that he joined almost two years later. The waterproof oilcloth that wraps its leather binding, the water stains that brown the pages nonetheless, the pencil calculations smudged into the endpapers—all these reveal the pocket-sized manual traveling to places where no shelter or inkwell is handy. Unevenly stitched-up pages testify in thread to the protectiveness inspired by belongings small enough to be worn against the skin. Separated by only a few layers of cloth, the book's wounds become an extension of the soldier's.

By the era of streetcars, riding was synonymous enough with reading for sci-fi to imagine the airships of the future equipped with in-flight newspapers.[33] Though the airships never materialized, the first airplane passengers were quick to notice "'inflight magazines' . . . conveniently located next to the motion sickness bags."[34] Advertisers largely abandoned in-flight magazines only once smartphones took away the captive audience of travelers who had misgauged how many pounds of paper would last a transatlantic flight.

If new kinds of commuting opened up time and space for reading, reciprocally printed matter helped the swelling ranks of office workers tolerate a long slog from home to work. It might not be too much of a stretch to claim that without books and newspapers, the Victorians would never have invented the suburb. We compare the web to an "information superhighway," but literal highways depend on commuting time filled by music or recorded speech. At the dawn of the MP3, about half of audiobooks in circulation were accessed on the cassette decks of commuters' cars.[35] In the 1970s, that historical sweet spot between the end of the *Chatterley* ban and the development of Sony's first Walkman, Georges Perec announced that "the true library of the people is the Metro."[36]

In 1994, as monitors began to edge photocopies off desks, the novelist E. Annie Proulx predicted that pleasure reading would stay on paper. "Nobody," Proulx declared, "is going to sit down and read a novel on a twitchy little screen. Ever."[37] Yet within a decade of her prediction, the emergence of unlimited text-messaging plans in Japan had the unintended consequence of creating a market for novels scrolled down a few eye-watering lines at a time. By 2008, five of the country's ten best-selling print books were cell-phone novels, composed on phone keypads and squinted at on miniature screens.[38] Only Proulx's technicality about "sitting down" held true, for these pleasures were taken standing. The cell-phone novel's natural habitat was the crowded Tokyo subway, in a straphanger's free hand.

In the early days of Tumblr, a photographer named Ourit Ben-Haim began to snap the backs of books swaying their way across the five boroughs. Her *Underground New York Public Library* proved a good place to get ideas for new reading material: every model a sandwich man. Later, a team of commuters took the name of @CoverSpy to note the books they saw in the hands of their fellow commuters, tweeting cover images along with capsule descriptions of the passenger reading them ("*Labour in Irish History*, James Connolly [M, 20s, glasses, black coat, brown cap, lost balance on train, C train]"; "*Grant*, Ron Chernow [M, 60s, blue windbreaker, gray beard, licking index finger before turning each page, 1 train]").

Told from the point of view of transportation, the history of mobile reading departs from both print and electronic book publishers' stories of progress. Instead of tracing changes in reading habits to successive technologies, we can see styles of reading changing in step with the times and places carved out by new infrastructures. Those new settings, in turn, welcomed new shapes and sizes of reading matter. Whether the legibility of a page depends on the presence of sunlight or the absence of glare, whether a book's cover hides the inside from prying eyes or a broadsheet allows two pairs of eyes to scan different sides of the same surface: the way each of these objects was carried changed the way readers carried themselves.

The more new times and places lent themselves to reading, the more rules needed to be imposed or self-imposed about what to read when. The golden age of print scheduled scale, whether weekly—Dickens's character Captain Cuttle "made it a point of duty to read none but very large books on a Sunday, as having a more staid appearance"[39]—or daily, as when the Earl of Chesterfield explained that "I converse with grave folios in the morning, while my head is clearest and my attention strongest: I take up less severe quartos after dinner; and at night I choose the mixed company and amusing chit-chat of octavos and duodecimos."[40] This eighteenth-century gentleman was measuring the passage of time by progressing from volumes as deskbound as an iMac to others as handy as a smartphone.

Keeping one book running for mornings while holding another in reserve for the afternoons became as crucial to Victorian gentleman scholars' routine as was eating bacon for breakfast and soup for supper. In his retirement, Gladstone rotated (in his own words) "Dr Langer's Roman History (in German) for morning reading, Virgil for afternoon, and a novel in the evening."[41] Virginia Woolf's father reveled in violating hourly *and* weekly norms when on April 24, 1870, he reported "spending a quiet Sunday morning in Birkbeck's smoking room—reading a novel."[42]

Asking when people read, though, is only one way to register books' entanglement with schedules. Other research tracks when people borrowed books that they may or may not have followed through with reading. One eighteenth-century library register shows more use in winter than summer and reveals that rural people "tended to take out books towards the end of the week, even when the library was open on Monday and Tuesday."[43] We could ask, even more obliquely, what people did and didn't notice about when they read. When do diarists register only on what day of the month they read a work, for example, and when do they specify the time of day?[44] Scrapbookers who paste in tickets from plays they attended rarely make a note of the show's hour, because everyone knows at what time a performance takes place. In contrast, an elderly Lady Trevelyan (born Hannah Macaulay) could still recall the place (the seaside resort Brighton), the year (1816), the season (summer), and the time (evening) when as a girl she'd listened to her brother Tom read aloud the interminable novel *Sir Charles Grandison*.

The beach book is marked by its banishment from daily working life. Hannah explains that "poetry and novels, except during Tom's holidays, were forbidden in the daytime, and stigmatised as 'drinking drams in the morning.'"[45] Their father's rules responded to the threat posed by cheap print's ubiquity and what we would call today its "always-on-ness": before the advent of sound recording, no need to warn your son against 10 a.m. symphonies. When the structuralist theorist Gérard Genette observed that texts lack tempo markings, he omitted to add that, also unlike music before the age of sound recording, print can be experienced in whatever time and place you choose—light permitting.[46]

From the age of the oil lamp to the age of the gas mantle, after-hours novel reading was considered the surest sign of insanity.[47] Early illustrators outfitted Don Quixote with a nightcap to signal that (as Burton Raffel translates it) "with virtually no sleep and so much reading he dried out his brain."[48] The candlelit pages of chivalric romances disrupt the biological rhythms that reassert themselves as soon as Don Quixote takes to the road, where darkness marks the end of each day and each chapter.

The genre being read mattered as much as the kind of person doing the reading—and the pace at which books were read mattered as much as the time of day at which that reading happened. Reading at the wrong time, at the wrong pace, by the wrong person continued to worry moralists even as the demographics of who counted as the wrong person shifted. By the eighteenth century, Cervantes's doddering old man was upstaged by the romance readers whom Samuel Johnson termed "the young, the ignorant, and the idle"—and, increasingly, the female. The night shift falls to women, as Don Quixote's shabby study changes into the boudoir of an aristocratic lady, who, after dressing for a ball (according to Rousseau's self-aggrandizing account)

began to read [*La Nouvelle Héloïse*] while waiting for the time [to leave]. At midnight she ordered [her servants] to get the horses ready and continued to read. They came to tell her that her horses were ready; she gave no answer. Seeing that she was forgetting herself, her [servants] came to notify her that it was two o'clock. "There is no rush yet," she said, still reading. Sometime afterward, because her watch had stopped, she rang to know what time it was. They told her that it was four o'clock. "Since that is so," she said, "it is too late to go to the ball, put up my horses." She had herself undressed and [spent] the rest of the night reading.[49]

I first encountered the anecdote in the work of pioneering book historian Robert Darnton, who used a trove of fan mail sent to Rousseau to reconstruct readers' responses to the novel. Replace "horse" with "car" and the scene Rousseau describes will be plausible to anyone who's ever sat in the driveway, removing the key from the ignition only once an audiobook reaches its end. When Amazon decided to strip the Kindle app of an on-screen clock, it followed Rousseau in making the breakdown of time-keeping gauge the reader's rapture. When the "reading mode" that followed disabled alerts and reminders, interrupting servants were definitively shown the door.[50]

In contrasting the unpunctual aristocrat with her servants who read only clocks, Rousseau slyly reversed eighteenth-century conduct literature's warning to servants against reading on their masters' time or tallow. Samuel Richardson boasted that as an autodidactic apprentice, he "took Care, that even my Candle was of my own purchasing, that I might not in the most trifling Instance make my Master a Sufferer."[51] Decades later, his 1747 novel *Clarissa* featured an aristocratic villain who sets fire to a house before laying the blame on "the carelessness of Mrs. Sinclair's cook-maid, who, having sat up to read the simple history of Dorastus and Faunia, when she should have been in bed, had set fire to an old pair of callicoe window-curtains."[52] Other characters believe the lie precisely because such accidents traditionally concretized the moral danger of servants' reading: burning the bed prefigured hellfire. Books at the wrong time scrambled natural rhythms as surely as books in the wrong hands upended the social order.

For that same reason, reading at the wrong time could bring the thrill of rebellion. In the last days of the Hapsburg empire, books tempted a small-town child named Nikola Tesla to stay up after his bedtime, until his father had to hide the family's candles. Years later, after growing up to become an electrical engineer, Tesla remembered scavenging for tallow to cast into candles with homemade wicks. All night, the aging inventor wrote in his memoir, "I would [plug] the keyhole and read, often till dawn when all others slept."[53] Snuggled under the covers while his parents snored, Tesla cradled the book as tenderly as a lover's body.

Considering media history alongside the history of the steam engine and the suburb suggests that the particular technology through which texts and images are disseminated matters less than larger-scale changes in the structure of daily lives. As one social critic has put it, we might tie the decline of pleasure reading to "the generalization of insecurity and economic precarity; the erosion of the separation between work and life; the decline of the home's integrity as a space external to the bustle of capitalist existence."[54] To understand what this means, consider those subway novel-readers. Now that cellular networks have penetrated underground, the same office worker who might have once used a presidential biography to while away the minutes of his commute might now use that time to answer work emails. His problem isn't the lack of the right reading device—print or electronic—but the work ethos, in the twenty-first century, that means that no one's ever really off the clock. Once in-flight wireless arrived, some workers were not only expected to travel long distances for their jobs but to spend the time in transit working too. Now "airplane mode" has become as metaphorical as the "library atmosphere" that Amtrak invoked in the heyday of the laptop.

Perhaps that's why, in the age of the backlit screen, we hope that the print reading that once flouted schedules can set them. Weeks after the launch of the iPhone 5, I went to a North London housing estate to meet an administrative assistant, just retired, who was a hundred pages into a well-creased movie tie-in paperback of Somerset Maugham's *The Painted Veil*. She'd never had time for fiction before, but her doctor blamed her insomnia on late-night screen time. She had joined the housing estate's book club, she explained, to break her habit of checking Facebook at night. Novel reading would provide her with an evening routine, lit by nothing more inflammatory than a bedside incandescent.

Then again, that reversal may be less drastic than it looks. As the books once expected to stimulate retrain to sedate, adults are granted what was, for more than a century, a toddler's prerogative. When nineteenth-century publishers invented the bedtime story, print began its slow march from a rule breaker to a schedule setter.[55] Only in the era of the adult coloring book, though, can readers of any age be bribed to sleep by print. When the University of Warwick launched a new online course, Literature and Mental Health, its syllabus promised not that Austen or Wordsworth will provide insight into the human mind, but rather that reading them will "calm" and "reassure."[56]

The transformation of print from a rousing wake-up call to something more like a blankie comes as part of a broader infantilization of reading. Digital-era observers have struggled to explain why so many American adults are reading literature meant for children. In 2012, 55 percent of young-adult books were purchased by buyers over seventeen, of whom a surprising 78 percent reported that the book wasn't intended as a gift.[57] Two years later, a Nielsen study attributed 80 percent of young-adult literature sales to over-seventeen readers.[58] Once, children peeked into their parents' copies of *The Joy of Sex*. Now, the balance of trade was reversing. The twentieth-century fear of teenagers' laying their hands on "mature content" gave way to a new anxiety about adults reading books written and marketed for teenagers.[59] As books went from stirring readers up to calming them down, so reading's relation to age changed as well. From an activity that speeds time up, turning teenagers into adults, reading has become a means of regression.

Nowhere is that truer than at bedtime. The BBC now advises insomniac listeners to "get stuck into a good book, practice meditation or have a relaxing bubble bath."[60] Like the doctor's recommendation, their advice has evidence behind it. In 2014, one clinical study suggested that reading electronically rather than on paper "can cause sleep deprivation and increase the risk of cancer." The study in question correlated the use of smartphones and iPads with lower levels of melatonin, the hormone that regulates sleepiness. Its absence is associated, as well, with breast, bowel, and prostate cancer.[61] A finer-grained comparison revealed that when participants did their bedtime reading on an iPad, their melatonin levels were lower than those who read either printed books or e-readers.[62] Once again, the study design is as telling as its results. The researchers weren't comparing *Good Night, Gorilla* with *Gone Girl*. Their focus was the delivery device. But of course, what might make printed books more relaxing than reading on an iPad might not be the medium itself but the fact that emails and alerts reminding us of the tasks that await us when we wake the next day don't pop up on our paperbacks.

If you care about the future of the deep, sustained engagement with lasting truths that a few books have long sparked in a few readers, then the threat you should be worried about isn't the Kindle. E-readers—hardware designed specifically for the reading of long-form, infrequently updated, purely textual content—remain one of Silicon Valley's most spectacular flops. From their peak of 23 million in 2011, e-reader sales have declined worldwide in each successive year, dwindling to less than a third of that in 2016. Devices that promised to revolutionize reading habits were quick to go bust (like the Sony e-reader launched in 2004 and retired a decade later), drive companies bankrupt (as seems likely if Barnes and Noble keeps taking losses on its Nook e-reader).[63]

But electronic reading thrives even as e-readers, on which the only reading matter is book length, turn out to have been a dead end. Ebook sales have risen steadily since 2015, with Amazon and self-published imprints increasingly dominating those sales. Now, the long-form, shelf-stable electronic texts that e-readers were designed to deliver are increasingly accessed through digital reading applications and other software programs accessed on internet-enabled devices whose primary purpose involves shorter and more ephemeral text. In 2017, 61 percent of American ebook readers reported accessing texts through a tablet, compared to 54 percent who reported accessing ebooks through an e-reader. Significant numbers also reported using Wi-Fi-equipped smartphones and laptops for the same purpose.[64]

In 2019, journalist Paul Greenberg noted that the average American spent 1,500-odd hours yearly on their smartphone. Searching for a benchmark that would convey the magnitude of those hours, he calculated that at average reading speed (280 words per minute), that same American could enjoy or at least endure Proust's *In Search of Lost Time*—twenty times every year.[65] It's a memorable metric. If you're old enough to think back to those distant days before your first smartphone, though, you may try and fail to remember those twenty-fold perusals of Proust. Just as one can calculate how many times the cars parked in Los Angeles can circle the world without actually lining Volvos up along the equator, Proust rereading appears here more as a measurement of absurd duration than as an activity in which one might realistically engage.

News articles with titles like "The Death of Books Has Been Greatly Exaggerated" regularly cite, as evidence for the health of printed books, consumers' distaste for their electronic equivalent.[66] Pbooks and ebooks, though, may not be the real antagonists. If you've been beating yourself up for reading fewer printed books, the culprit is unlikely to be ebooks, much less e-readers. The real competition comes from the same corner that it did in the print era: image-heavy chunks of disposable, browsable ephemera.[67] Our ancestors called them "the paper."

We know that the Sunday paper arose as a secular way of marking the distinction between work and leisure time, but it's easier to forget that religious reading itself arose in part as a way of filling the long hours when work was forbidden. One 1896 article on "Sunday Reading," for example, declares that "in the prohibition of games and of the usual activities of young life upon that day, reading becomes almost the only resource." The point is not that goody-goody books crowd out exciting romances, but that sitting still, with the book as a kind of seat belt, takes the place of active work and play.[68] Charlotte Yonge's contrast between girls and boys morphs here into a contrast between children and adults. In both cases, you read because there's nothing else to do.

The overrepresentation of the very old and very young in the reading public; the emergence of the mass-circulation newspaper in the nineteenth century thanks to suburbs linked by commuter train; fiction's persistent alliance with bed, beach, and beyond; the centuries-old fear of housewives' fiction-fueled imaginations—all these reflect the vacuums that print once rushed in to fill. In each case, making room for reading has turned out to hinge less on finding the right device—or even on shutting off the wrong device—than on carving out some digital-age equivalent to those negative spaces.

If you value the union of opposites brokered (sometimes but not always) by long-form, long-term reading—emotional absorption with intellectual reflection, inwardness with empathy, the capacity to withdraw from those around us while remaining attuned to distant minds—then the book may no longer be the only place to look. If we think of printed paper not as an inert collectible but as a cue or catalyst, then fetishizing the wood pulp and thread or glue onto which attentiveness, curiosity, and imagination have sometimes piggybacked means looking in the wrong place. More useful might be exploring what new—or old but forgotten—ways of circulating and sharing and responding to words might allow those habits to flourish.

We might find one example in the work of the great utopian socialist writer, printer, and designer William Morris. In the same year that Dewey was celebrating the mobilization of the book, Morris pointed out dryly that easy to carry means hard to hold. "A small book," he explained, shortly after the pocket lexicon returned from the Civil War in one piece (though verging on two pieces whenever the tenuous binding finally gave way),

> seldom does lie quiet, and you have either to cramp your hand by holding it, or else to put it on the table with a paraphernalia of matters to keep it down, a table-spoon on one side, a knife on another. . . . Whereas, a big folio lies quiet and majestic on the table, waiting kindly till you please to come to it, with its leaves flat and peaceful, giving you no trouble of body, so that your mind is free to enjoy the literature which its beauty enshrines.[69]

What Morris says of the hand could equally well be applied to the eye. The type size that makes a book fit into a pocket or reticule can also make it illegible for all but the most clear-sighted readers. (You may have dithered between staggering under a backpack full of large-print hardbacks or squinting at fine print that straggles off into the gutter of onionskin page spreads.) And as Kindle ads' attacks on the iPad's susceptibility to glare remind us, the ease with which words can be carried to the

beach makes them harder to read there. At the end of the twentieth century, Frederick Kilgour, the creator of the first online
union catalog that made it possible for any computer user to
search information about the holdings of multiple libraries,
described the book as "an artifact that is portable—or at least
transportable."[70] How to weight ease of carrying against ease of
use remains an open question in the twenty-first.

A shell game shuttles effort around the user's body. Folios
save the eyes at the expense of the back; paperbacks spare shoulders but crane necks. Human decisions, as much as the laws
of physics, ensure that the same technologies that promise to
cure our ills can cause others. Currently, for example, despite
the possibilities offered in principle by digital text that can be
expanded or converted into voice, private companies' digital
rights management strategies are making texts less accessible to
disabled readers than they were in the era that stretched from
the early-nineteenth-century invention of Braille to the rise of
the audiobook recorded on vinyl.[71]

Yet what Morris questioned was something even more basic
than small books' practicality: Were convenience and efficiency
desirable in the first place? His 1896 romance *The Well at the
World's End* envisioned a book readable only when laid open on
a particular stone altar at a particular place in a particular forest.
Literary critic Jerome McGann has shown that Morris's own
press deliberately made books "hard to read," jamming up the
works to force readers to pause long enough to notice their look
and feel.[72] In place of conspicuous consumption, his high-end,
high-volume volumes offered conspicuous inconvenience.[73]

The same unwieldiness that enforces a slowdown also limits
the situations in which a book can be used and the company in

which it's accessed. As far as convenience goes, the eleventh-century tax survey known as the Domesday Book, kept in a special chest with three different locks whose keys were divided among three people, has less in common with a Penguin paperback than with an encrypted website that can be accessed only by entering a code sent to the user's cell phone. The Domesday Book looks more like the paperback, but functions more like the website.

Immobility doesn't have to mean monumentality. No one ever revered the yellow pages tethered to telephone booths. But by restoring the sense of occasion that he associated with medieval manuscripts, Morris hoped to forestall the always-on reading that we equate with the smartphone but that he blamed on cheap print. Like familiarity, ubiquity breeds contempt.

What John Plotz terms Morris's "experiments against portability" go well beyond substituting big books for small.[74] The media to which Morris gravitated—tapestries designed to match the size of a particular wall, or wallpaper that would be destroyed if pried away—reject the convenience of easel paintings that can be rehung, engravings that can be stashed in a drawer, and books that can be slipped into a pocket. Morris provides one corrective to the technoboosterism that Google and Amazon inherit from Dewey. In distinguishing ease of access from quality of engagement, *The Well at the World's End* reminds us that chained books may set imaginations free.

INTERLEAF: PLE

ONE AFTERNOON IN the reign of the iPhone 4, I uncurled
two hardbacks in my book bag. As I slid the strap over
magazines thumbed in doctors' waiting rooms, the fine print on
Hunching over my laptop to Google "back pain," I learned
legislate the weight of children's schoolbags. Faced with a study
the average child, a bill now capped bookbags at 10 percent of the
the laptop's clamshell might be worsening my back. I sat an external
its electronic equivalent, and sat myself on a flat, matte edition of
catalog, whose oversize pages made me hope for stability, only
Adjusting the tottering stack, I was newly grateful to have shelves
in shape (one reason Jeff Bezos made books the guinea pig for his
need to prop up one leg of a table, there's bound to be *some* book
But ejecting my laptop from my lap turned out not to stem the
reading. My leg spasmed the moment I lowered myself into what had
Faced with a choice between standing or lying flat, I found myself
pages projected onto the ceiling. Pacing the room while I held a
I'd thought of books as what you picked up when you were
running laps, an adult who took novels to sickbeds. But now that
from the familiar geometry of bound pages on a table facing a body
to more and more doctors, my books abandoned their usual waist
teetered on cinder blocks, like the stilettos I could no longer wear
of Galen Cranz's *The Chair* (1998) spread-eagled on top of its glass.
I learned from Cranz, an architect as well as a practitioner of
the metonymy "chairman"; hence the shock value of Gandhi's

ASE LAY FLAT

my back, unfurled my neck, and sandwiched my laptop between my shoulder, my spine gave. Let's pass quickly over the rest: the pill bottles.

that in 2006, India had become the first country in the world to finding that the average backpack weighed almost half as much as weight of a schoolchild.[1] I learned, too, that my goosenecking over monitor on a squat Portuguese-English dictionary superseded by Emily Dickinson's envelope poems (I'd tried a Robert Motherwell to realize that most art books are cursed with slippery covers). full of cheap, ubiquitous objects that are both relatively uniform mail-order business: their box-ability) and varied in size (if you in your possession that fits).[2]

pain. I stopped biking, stopped drinking, and eventually stopped once been the most comfortable piece of furniture, a cushioned chair. without a lap to rest a book on. Flat on the floor, I fantasized about volume open, I craved a third hand with which to annotate.

too weak to do anything else: a kid who hid in study hall to avoid reading made me ill, illness stopped me from reading. Or, at least, on a chair. Instead, I was learning new ways to read. As I shuttled height for higher and lower perches. Higher, because my desk soon myself. And lower, once I lay underneath a coffee table with a copy

the Alexander Technique, that chairs connote prestige. Hence decision to sit on the floor. The International Civil Rights Center

and Museum in Greensboro, North Carolina, enshrines the
boundary between the bar where blacks stood and the counter
    Yet standing can also confer power. In Romance languages,
is what humans tell dogs. Looming over a seminar table, I struck
Prevented from sitting at their level, I saw words like "authoritarian"
was true; no longer able to twist my body like a sunflower to feign
    The icon for disability is a wheelchair: the paradigmatic cripple
almost as much stigma. Flight attendants treated my unbuckled seat
reading wouldn't be remarked upon: rush-hour subways, checkout
1793 painting showed the Jacobin martyr Marat dying in a bathtub,
dermatitis herpetiformis, Marat had been soaking in vinegar while
the-tub writing trays. Their buyers may have been missing the point.
but reading with one hand kept dry while the other soaps enables
you can't take notes; sometimes, one wants to be prevented from
    My reading positions wouldn't have seemed so strange in earlier
to rest their scrolls; in an age when adults regularly read aloud,
reading as a healthy exercise for body and mind: it expanded
once the unfurled scroll gave way to the folded codex did readers
stood at attention before the vellum that they were illuminating,
of safer candles and to the shrinking of trim sizes. Previously
treason could now be slipped into a pocket. Readers since then
broadsheet, tucking their faces into a laptop's fold, and screening
    A Bible feels different when it inhabits a pulpit or a reader's lap;
the newsstand or spread on the breakfast table. Whether the reader's
electronic object itself, but on the surfaces that support her body
the designer Craig Mod proposed to customize fonts not just for
eye: "Bed (close to face)," "Knee (medium distance from face)," and
    The rise of literacy can be told as a story about desk height and
physically supporting a book, unless one outsources that work to a

chairs occupied during the 1960 sit-in that breached Woolworths'
where whites sat.

the word for "seat" comes from the same root as "sedative." "Sit"
students dumb: the tallest person in the room is usually the loudest.

sprout on my students' evaluations. I'd like to think the opposite
interest in other speakers, I actually had to listen.

sits while others stand. The reverse, though, turned out to prompt
belt like an open straitjacket. I brought books to places where upright
lines. In museums, I stood staring at portraits of sitters. David's
flanked by an inkstand and a pool of his own blood. To treat his
answering the mail. The painting's success boosted demand for over-
Rousseau called pornography "books one reads with one hand,"
subtler pleasures. I keep books by the bath because it's the one place
multitasking.

eras. The Romans needed no chair to sit on or table on which
standing allowed the voice to project. Doctors recommended
the lungs, strengthened the arms, and stretched the back. Only
began to hinge at the waist as well. Medieval monks perched or
but eighteenth-century readers bedded books thanks to the rise
as large as a 1950s mainframe, a text containing pornography or
have returned to the vertical, scanning billboards, hiding behind a
their face behind a phone like some court lady's fan.

a newspaper, when its headlines are read while loitering opposite
neck or back bears the brunt depends not just on the printed or
and her reading material. In the early days of tablet computing,
differently sized devices, but also for different distances from the
"Breakfast (far from face)," the latter in order to keep crumbs away.[3]
spectacle design. Reading, we all know, takes effort. But so does
piece of furniture. The historian Erich Schon points out that before

around 1800, books were most often depicted in hands or on knees.
contact with the text dwindle to an occasional touch of the finger:

By extension, the intellectual work—or lack thereof—elicited by
lack thereof—of the bodies that hold them, even of the furniture
sprawls on a sofa or lolls at the hairdresser's; a fine snow of hair
Goriot to "you who are holding this book in your fair white hand,
declared, "I have no faith in reading that is compatible with an arm-
writing desk over those that manifested spinelessness.[4]

Dickensian clerks perched at high stools, like McMansion
though, bodies and papers changed places in the office. The women
while vertical filing forced papers that had once rested flat onto their
slumping in drawers."[5]

As copying and filing became women's work, writing literature
Hemingway explained in a 1950 letter that "writing and travel
up." Nabokov told a *Playboy* interviewer that "I generally start the
on, when I feel gravity nibbling at my calves, I settle down in a
finally, when gravity begins climbing up my spine, I lie down on
containing the interview was read.[6] At the turn of the millennium,
posture in which they peed. Donald Rumsfeld worked standing,
the same pneumatic lifts used in chairs.

Centuries before the Kindle became the device of choice for
baby in the other hand), labor-saving devices aimed to take books
Even the "index" takes its name from the second digit, used to hold
designed Ferris wheel–like contraptions in which each volume
bookshelves that spin the desired book into arm's reach; lecterns
such 1588 machine promised to spare "those who are indisposed
on the contrary, we adjust our chairs in relation to a fixed-height

At the end of the nineteenth century, one early adopter
Octave Uzanne pointed out, "forces our bodies into various
it constrains us to acquire a certain dexterity in the art of turning

Only once books came to rest on tables did the reader's bodily
eyes replaced hands.
different literary genres can be made visible by the uprightness—or
that holds those bodies. In eighteenth-century paintings, the reader
powder dusted the pages. In 1835, Balzac addressed his novel *Father*
you who sink down in your soft easy chair." When Lucy Soulsby
chair," she was privileging those kinds of reading that required a

dwellers at a breakfast bar. At the end of the nineteenth century,
taking over formerly male-dominated office jobs subsided into chairs,
edge, thanks to new cabinets guaranteed to prevent "sagging or

retained its manly aura only by eschewing comfortable chairs.
broaden your ass if not your mind and I like to write standing
day at a lovely old-fashioned lectern I have in my study. Later
comfortable armchair alongside an ordinary writing desk; and
a couch"—the same position, perhaps, in which that magazine
the position in which men wrote remained as distinctive as the
and Dick Cheney bought an adjustable-height desk propelled by

nursing mothers (one-handed swiping makes it possible to hold a
off readers' hands. Bookmarks began their life as prosthetic fingers.[7]
one page open while flipping to another. Renaissance inventors
rides flat on a tray, open to just the right page; lazy Susan–like
equipped with angle brackets and height-adjustable screws. One
and tormented by gout" the trouble of lifting their books. Today,
reading surface.
proposed a solution to back pain: sound recording. Reading,
fatiguing attitudes. If we are reading one of our great newspapers
and folding the sheets; if we hold the paper wide open it is not

long before the muscles of tension are overtaxed, and finally, if leaves and turning them one after another, ends by producing an worried that the solution would soon give rise to a new problem: so with the phonography yet to be, the aurists will begin to dictated to secretaries, so audiobooks automate the eighteenth-master's chair.

Today, no bigger bait and switch exists than what parents do when reading with snuggles, only to plunge him or her into a lifetime of got read aloud to too. Scholars debate how representative of fourth-at seeing another reader staring at a page but making no sound. (ratherthanrunningthemtogetherlikethis) allowed readers to parse readers continued to move their mouths, as children do today. Nilo factories routinely paid a "lector" to read aloud to them: Montecristo weeks and months.

My own story has that most bookish of structures, a happy binder with one foot propped on a book. For the yellow pages Microsoft manual. Now that abdominal curls have unscrolled my WebMD.com.

I learned something more basic, though, that no ergonomics coached me to stop aiming for the perfect posture that girls once to be flexible. Readers can likewise learn when to read in print and slowly, when to search an encyclopedia and when to have their

we address ourselves to the book, the necessity of cutting the
enervated condition very distressing in the long run." But he also
"Just as oculists have multiplied since the invention of journalism,
abound."[8] As Siri's ladylike voice resurrects the days when bosses
century servants who read aloud, standing discreetly behind their

they read aloud to a baby. Hook your darling on books by associating
tête-à-têtes with books. For most of human history, though, adults
century readers St. Augustine was when he reported his shock
Even once the new convention of inserting spaces between words
text without having to sound it out syllable by syllable, medieval
Cruz's play *Anna in the Tropics* reminds us that workers in Cuban cigar
cigars honored the Dumas novel that they heard over the course of

ending. An occupational therapist taught me to sit on a three-ring
pictured in her yellowing diagrams, I substituted an outdated
spine, I can finally curl up with a good book. Or, at least, with

textbook could have taught me. The occupational therapist also
learned by balancing books on their heads. Instead, she taught me
when to opt for digital, when to read quickly and when to read
souls searched by a poem.

Chapter 4

PRESCRIBED READING

I N 2005, a Cardiff psychiatrist named Neil Frude saw his patients waiting months to be prescribed antidepressants, and years to receive talk therapy. He noticed, as well, that they were filling those days and months of waiting with furtive forays to the self-help section of the bookstore or, in the privacy of a home or library, with what was then coming to be known as Googling. Of the more than 100,000 books on sale that offered psychiatric advice in layman's language, at least some seemed to help. If randomized trials could identify which books those were, Frude realized, doctors without specialized psychiatric training would be able to recommend them.

Soon, "recommend" ratcheted up to "prescribe." In NHS Wales's Book Prescription program, any primary-care physician who diagnoses mild to moderate depression can scribble a title on a prescription pad. The patient takes the torn-off sheet not to the pharmacy but to her local library, where it gets exchanged for a copy of *Overcoming Depression* or *The Feeling Good Handbook*. Now that depression is only one of over a dozen conditions treated, libraries across Wales stock *Mind Over Mood*, *Overcoming Traumatic Stress*, *Getting Better Bit(e) by Bit(e)*, and *The Worry Cure*. Those made anxious by all that required reading can choose between *Stop Worrying About Your Health!* and *An Introduction to Coping with Health Anxiety: A Books on Prescription Title*.[1]

By 2011, doctors in Wales were issuing 30,000 book prescriptions a year.[2] Whether or not those books were ever opened, many of them at least got as far as the circulation desk. By 2013, a third of libraries' top ten most borrowed titles were self-help books.[3] A public library system suffering even more drastic budget cuts than the health service was in no position to turn away the foot traffic, funding, and legitimacy that Book Prescription supplied. No wonder that in 2013, Books on Prescription began to spread beyond Wales. England's Reading Well initiative was launched by a nonprofit rather than its own health service, but the doctors who participated were paid by the NHS. Within three months, English libraries had lent over 100,000 copies of the prescribed titles—20,000 more than *Fifty Shades of Grey*.[4]

It's logical enough for an underresourced health system to outsource the work of expensive medical professionals to underpaid librarians and cheap books. What might come as more of a surprise is that self-help isn't the only genre that the National Health Service is endorsing. The second branch of Reading Well, Mood-Boosting Books, recommends fiction, poetry, and memoirs. MBB's annual lists jumble fiction whose characters are anxious or depressed (such as Mark Haddon's *A Spot of Bother*) with books that lack direct representations of mental illness but are likely to jerk a tear or a laugh. Still others represent characters comforted by reading: a novel enrolls its characters in a reading group (*The Guernsey Literary and Potato Peel Pie Society* by Mary Ann Shaffer and Annie Barrows); an autobiography chronicles a footballer's journey toward literacy (*Tackling Life* by Charlie Oatway).

This leads to some strange shelf-fellows. In the same year as the Nobel Committee, Mood-Boosting Books honored Alice Munro's *Too Much Happiness*. The first honor seems a lot easier to understand than the second, since Munro's collection of mood-killing stories turns, specifically, on the often disturbing power dynamics brokered by books. One story's naked heroine is tricked into reading aloud to a fully clothed man. Another story depicts a postoperative radio announcer, eyes bandaged, listening to books read aloud by a sinisterly unidentified woman. A third protagonist "hated to hear the word 'escape' used about fiction. She might have argued, not just playfully, that it was real life that was the escape." Also in *Too Much Happiness*, a character writes a book of short stories with "some title like a how-to book," *How Are We to Live*. That character's "mission in life is to make people feel uncomfortable."[5] One wonders whether the person who added Munro's collection to the list of Mood-Boosting Books got past its title page. While the Mood-Boosting program enlists fiction to alleviate anxiety and depression, Munro casts literature as an unsettler.

The merging of self-help and literature under the umbrella of Reading Well makes visible, as in a caricature, the double transformation that long-form print literature has undergone since the turn of the millennium. Literature has become medicalized, as the act of reading has been placed in the service of mental and physical well-being, but also institutionalized, as state-funded agencies are weighing in ever more systematically on whether to read and what to read. You might explain this second change as a corollary of the infantilization described in Chapter 3: at the same moment when bedtime stories spread from toddlers to adults, assigned reading extended its reach from schoolchildren to adult NHS patients.

The convergence of psychiatric treatment and textual engagement might suggest that these otherwise very different activities are following a similar trajectory. Psychiatry, once focused on the surprising revelations that could emerge in the therapist-patient conversation, and reading, once experienced as a serendipitous encounter between a person and a book, are both being automated and instrumentalized under pressure from cash-strapped governments. Yet you might also see reading and psychiatry moving in opposite directions: the very moment when psychiatrists have come to subordinate form to content (assuming that it doesn't matter whether the treatment is delivered by a therapist or a book or an app) is also the moment when policy makers are shifting their interest in literature from content to form (where once governments focused on censoring books whose topics included sex or violence, now they're just as eager to promote the experience of long-form literary reading, regardless of subject matter).

Bibliotherapy might seem like a boon not only to the health industry, but also to the book industry. The foot traffic, funding, and legitimacy that Reading Well supplies are sorely needed in a country that lost 343 libraries between 2010 and 2016. A crude economic calculation would make book prescription look like a win-win benefiting not just patients but taxpayers, and perhaps (however unintentionally) benefiting books. Library systems gain new patrons when doctors send patients through their doors. Literature reaches new readers every time a patient picks up a novel or a memoir en route to the circulation desk: come for *Feel the Fear . . . and Do It Anyway*, stay for *The Shining*.

For libraries as for beleaguered booklovers, an ally with as much clout as a national health service can only be welcome. Yet turning a bookshelf into a medicine cabinet raises troubling questions about why exactly a society should value reading, and which professions are authorized to measure that value.

From a medical vantage, books' selling points are largely negative: the money they don't cost, the side effects they don't produce, the addictions that they don't engender—all these allow them to beat out drugs and talk therapy alike. Unlike the antidepressants taken by one out of seven Americans and one out of six Britons, reading can't increase weight or decrease libido.[6] It doesn't even trigger nausea, unless you happen to be in the car.

Compared to one-on-one counseling, meanwhile, bibliotherapy looks absurdly cost-effective—for while randomized trials suggest that therapists outperform books by a narrow margin, books underbid therapists by a much wider one. A 2012 study that compared anxiety sufferers stuck on a therapist's waiting list to those prescribed self-help books found that the latter fared better but cautioned that "comparison of self-help with therapist-administered treatments revealed a significant difference in favor of the latter."[7] Translation: a book does worse than a therapist, but better than nothing. And for Brits enrolled in an NHS suffering from cuts as for the 3 million Americans who lack health insurance, nothing is what many sufferers would otherwise get.

As anomalous as therapeutic claims are within the history of books, they're perfectly consistent with a decades-long attempt to automate mental health. For most of the twentieth century, psychodynamic therapy took the therapist-patient relationship as its building block. The mere fact of human interaction mattered more than its content—rather as some believe that the power of print lies less in its message than the attention and focus that it elicits.

More recently, though, insurers' interest in cutting costs has conspired with researchers' interest in protocols that can be measured and replicated to favor short-term, standardized methods such as cognitive behavioral therapy. Books take this trajectory to its logical conclusion. If your aim is less to help patients explore the underlying causes of their condition than to offer step-by-step instructions for managing it, then who cares whether the exercises emanate from a mouth, a manual, or a smartphone app?[8]

Still, bibliotherapy pioneer Frude acknowledges that "'off-the-peg' treatments offered by self-help manuals" won't help "many people whose problems demand a more personal and a more bespoke treatment."[9] "Off the peg" is British for "off the rack": the analogy casts psychodynamic therapy as a luxury good, no more accessible to the masses than Savile Row tailoring. Books on Prescription launched across England in the same year that American universities like mine rolled out their first MOOCs, or massive open online courses. Frude's comparison of Books on Prescription to one-size-fits-most mass-market clothes echoes the populist logic used to market MOOCs. Both scale up an activity whose face-to-face version lies out of reach of the masses. Both also emphasize content delivery at the expense of the interpersonal give-and-take that goes on around the seminar table or in the consulting room. In the same way that lectures lend themselves more to online delivery than do courses involving discussion or hands-on projects, so cognitive behavioral therapy—broken down into discrete, standardized exercises—proves more adaptable than psychodynamic therapy to the impersonality of the book.[10]

But just as some students may find it tempting to ignore instructions delivered through a screen, Frude acknowledges that not all patients follow through with their assigned reading. At best, bibliotherapy works for those highly literate patients who are already "familiar with the process of following a structured 'recipe' in a book (as in a cookbook or a DIY manual)."[11] Just as anyone who follows the instructions in a cookbook will end up with a cake, he explains, a patient who uses the book as prescribed will end up with control over their emotions.

Since 2011, though, something has happened to Frude's analogy. If you're hungry today, a book isn't what you turn to. A long historical view suggests that culinary know-how is coming full circle: the cookbooks that emerged when the splintering of extended families prevented girls from watching their grandmothers bake may disappear again once YouTube eliminates the need to translate sight and touch into words. And once cookbooks go the way of the yellow pages, self-help books may not be far behind. Self-help has already joined romance and erotica as one of the earliest genres to sell well in electronic form: no one wants to advertise her alcoholism or codependency to anyone who glimpses the hardback she's carrying on the subway. What ebooks were to print, apps may soon be to ebooks: Epicurious.com has found its psychiatric counterpart in the interactive cognitive-behavioral exercises offered by websites such as Living Life to the Full (www.llttf .com) or Moodgym (www.moodgym.com.au).[12] As the book automates the therapist, so cognitive behavioral apps may soon underbid print. Meanwhile, health-care providers must bet on the medium—therapist, book, or app—being incidental to the content delivered.

Books on Prescription doesn't just reflect the evolution of psychiatry or the politics of health-care funding. Paradoxically enough, the shift to self-help books also responds to the rise of digital media. The turnstile of a specialized library once separated doctors from laypeople. But now that second-guessing your diagnosis doesn't require finding a table sturdy enough to hold some multivolume medical dictionary, the question becomes less whether patients will read than what. Pew surveys reveal that almost three-quarters of American adults use the internet for health-related searches.[13]

In 2016, Google reported that one out of every hundred uses of its searches involved medical symptoms; an independent estimate puts one out of twenty searches about health.[14] The following year, its search engine began redirecting anyone who typed or dictated "depression" into a mobile device to a diagnostic quiz.[15] Prompting users to tap "check if you're clinically depressed," Google blurred the distinction between checking a box on-screen and "checking" in the sense of "diagnosing." And once advertising vendors get into the act, doctors' intervention in patients' reading begins to look less like an innovation than like a rearguard action. Even if prescribed books go in one ear and out the other, they may at least crowd out pop-ups touting miracle cures.

If the medicalization of reading seems like a logistical step in the history of psychiatry, the alignment of self-help books with literature seems at first glance like a break from the history of reading. In fact, one of the earliest genres of self-help was the conduct book warning against too much novel reading. The inventor of the modern advice book, the aptly named Samuel Smiles, compared indulging in fiction to "dram-drinking." Books, Smiles warned, could never teach as much as the "life-education daily given in our homes, in the streets, behind counters, in workshops, at the loom and the plough, in counting-houses and manufactories." Selves could be helped "by work more than by reading— . . . life rather than literature, action rather than study."[16]

Smiles's *Self-Help* expanded for mass-distributed print a speech called "The Education of the Working Classes" that he delivered in person to a mutual improvement society, the MOOC of the day. In the book-length version, Smiles's assertion that "many of our most energetic and useful workers have been but sparing readers" seems to sit oddly alongside exemplary biographies of men inspired by childhood reading. A twelve-year-old progresses through the *Encyclopaedia Britannica* from A to Z after finishing his work at the counting-house, a warehouse boy defies the master who "warned him against too much reading," and "a poor gardener's boy" explains how he had managed to read Newton's *Principia* in Latin: "One needs only to know the twenty-four letters of the alphabet in order to learn everything else that one wishes."[17] Smiles's own book, available to anyone with access to a library or secondhand shop, replaced live advice from lectures and sermons. But Smiles drew a sharp distinction between educational nonfiction—such as encyclopedias, mathematical treatises, and self-help books—and literature consumed for pleasure. The former was to the latter as vegetables are to dessert.

There's nothing new about the NHS's assumption that novels affect the body and mind. But for most of the Gutenberg era, that effect was rarely thought to be for the better. Mood-Boosting Books reverses half a millennium's worth of campaigns *against* fiction waged first by churches, then by schools, and, eventually, by the public libraries founded in the nineteenth century that rationed the number of novels a borrower could take out but allowed all-you-can-read essay borrowing. Doctors provided all three institutions with expert backup. In Cervantes's Spain, printing allowed compilations of traditional romances to spread beyond the elite audiences that had once listened to them read aloud or been able to afford to access them in manuscript. The barber who would have been the only medical professional in Don Quixote's village burns those printed versions in the hope of saving his friend's "dried-out brain." The Romantics who thought that madmen were the greatest poets sometimes tarred fiction readers with the same brush: Goethe's novel *The Sorrows of Young Werther*, they pointed out, prompted copycat suicides.

Indeed, well into the nineteenth century, experts were likelier to think that fiction reading caused madness than cured it. A doctor warned in 1806 that reading "affects the organs of the body, and relaxes the tone of the nerves." As late as 1877, another expert "could tell of one young woman of my acquaintance, of fine education," "who gratified a vitiated taste for novel-reading till her reason was overthrown, and she has, in consequence, been for several years an inmate of an insane asylum."[18] If these professionals had time traveled forward, the biggest surprise to them might not have been antidepressants, but the NHS-sponsored alliance of fiction and self-help books.

The same printed books now tasked with curing the mind are also expected to heal eyes and backs. "You need a real book in your hand," one independent bookseller recently told a *New York Times* reporter, "the computer screen just hurts."[19] Earlier, though, it was books that were assumed to hurt hands, along with eyes, stomach, and pretty much every other body part. Long before 1949, when the term "ergonomics" was coined, doctors blamed reading for health hazards including (to quote one 1621 list of diagnoses by Richard Burton) "gouts, catarrhs, rheums, wasting, indigestion, bad eyes, stone, and colick, crudities, oppilations, vertigo, winds, consumptions and all such diseases as come by overmuch sitting" or (according to another expert in 1795) "weakening of the eyes, heat rashes, gout, arthritis, hemorrhoids, asthma, apoplexy, pulmonary disease, indigestion, blocking of the bowels, nervous disorder, migraines, epilepsy, hypochondria and melancholy." The comprehensiveness of the lists may have been tongue in cheek, but any of the individual items would have been familiar to a doctor. When Wordsworth imagined a reader being told "Up! Up! my Friend, and quit your books; / Or surely you'll grow double," the physical danger of doubling over—or just gaining weight—symbolized the duplicity of virtual experience.[20]

No sooner did the new infrastructures whose development we saw in Chapter 3 make reading convenient than it began to look dangerous—as harmful to the eyes and brain as sandwich munching was to the digestion. "Observe the passengers in the train," thundered one antebellum American moralist, "before all eyes, young and old, spectacled and otherwise, there oscillates some kind of printed page. Opportunity for fresh air is lost at the stopping-places, while the eyes are eagerly strained and worried over the plot of some novel."[21] The physical dangers of eyestrain concretize the mental dangers of distractedness.

By 1863, Isaac Ray, the superintendent of the Butler Hospital in Providence, Rhode Island, and a founder of the American Psychiatric Association, had used the latest medical methods to pinpoint reading as the source of "cerebral disorder," " irritability," and "abnormal erythism which often terminates in overt disease."[22] Ray attributed Americans' growing propensity for insanity and suicide to their "increasing fondness for light reading, especially such as is addressed to the emotions and the passions"—that is, to the very imaginative fiction that Mood-Boosting Books would later deploy as therapy.[23] Fiction was both cause of Americans' poor mental health—because "excessive indulgence in novel-reading necessarily enervates the mind"—and an effect of "a feverish pulse, a disturbed digestion, and irritable nerves" that created the "craving for an intense and exciting literature."[24]

Along with insanity came insomnia. The fears about nighttime reading that Chapter 3 traces culminated in one 1867 expert's caution that bedding a book could "injure your eyes, your brain, your nervous system." Cue the other under-the-blankets activity blamed for blindness. Ray had warned that "violent emotions thrill through the bodily frame" of fiction readers, whose habits resulted in "debasing effects constantly assisted by the habit of self-indulgence"—that is, of what would later come to be called masturbation.[25] Reading, too, threatened to upstage the mess and tedium of human contact with solipsistic fantasies.

Worse, textual stimuli could blot out the real world alto-gether. In 1889, one journalist compared books to drinks, dredging up his most scientific language to explain that just as alcoholism leads to "excessive fattening round the heart, and weak action of the heart in consequence," so "the habit of exciting novel-reading leads to fatty degeneration of the liter-ary mind,—*i.e.*, to an unhealthy and spasmodic action of the imagination." Another expert compared the pleasures of fic-tion reading to "the dram of the drunkard, creating a diseased craving for more."[26] To some, the book resembled the bottle; to others, a viper. In 1874, the *Methodist* magazine asked, "What is the presence of a poisonous reptile in a house to that of a poisonous book on our publishers' list?" At the other end of the cultural spectrum, the plot of Wilde's *The Picture of Dorian Gray* (1890) hinges on a "poisonous book," whose immoral sentences "produced in the mind of the lad, as he passed from chapter to chapter, a form of reverie, a malady."

As alcohol began to face competition from addictive phar-maceuticals, the fiction that had once been compared to drink came to be compared more often to pills. By 1894 a journalist observing modern readers' "physical need for novels" explained that "as in the case of all other sedatives, there comes to the per-son who is accustomed to use fiction to soothe his mind, a pos-itive craving for novels." And lest you think that his emphasis on the soothing nature of reading foreshadows the use of books to treat anxiety a century later, note that he saw the calming nature of fiction as a reason to throw it away. As he pointed out, "the very last thing which the man who uses novels as a sedative wants is to keep the volumes on his shelves. He would as soon think of keeping empty medicine bottles."[27]

If certain genres of book counted as mind-altering substances, why not regulate their sale? Decades before alcohol
and tobacco were ruled off-limits to the young, novels were
forbidden to under-sixteens. In 1883, the New York State Leg-
islature debated whether to fine "any person who shall sell, loan,
or give to any minor under sixteen years of age any dime novel
or book of fiction, without first obtaining the written consent
of the parent or guardian of such a minor."[28] Unsuccessful in
New York, a similar law passed three years later in Massachu-
setts, forbidding minors from buying "criminal news, police
reports, or accounts of criminal deeds, or pictures and stories
of lust and crime."[29] Teenagers needed to be protected. The 1901
expert who worried that it sapped "the power of concentration,
of attention, of memory [for a boy] to mope about the house
and to be eternally bending his back and straining his eyes over
the printed pages of a book" blamed print for the very vices
that reading is now expected to combat.[30] A 1916 commentator
added that "those children who prefer to stay at home and read
a good book when all the others are out and play[ing] can be
suspected of using reading as a sedative."[31] To childproof your
house, the bookcase needed to be locked as firmly as the medicine cabinet.

Today, on the contrary, the absence of printed stories is seen
as a threat to children's health. In 2014, the American Academy of Pediatrics enjoined pediatricians to recommend reading
aloud with the same authority with which it endorsed car seats.
Screen is to page as formula is to mother's milk. When my son
was an infant, I fretted as much about his access to books as to
breasts. Some parents start worrying even earlier. *With Love: A*

Book to Be Read to Your Child in Utero and Beyond outdoes Baby Einstein to produce a Fetus Shakespeare.

How exactly, though, did scientists' and policy makers' new faith in books replace the centuries-old suspicions that dogged them? Perhaps the explanation is that the first generation to accede to mass literacy was also the last for which the book had been the default communications medium. As other media began to challenge print's monopoly on popular entertainment, in other words, novels came to look like a lesser evil. In 1916, when cinema seemed to be on the verge of crowding out books, the clergyman Samuel Crothers coined the term "bibliotherapy," positing tongue in cheek that "a book may be a stimulant or a sedative or an irritant or a soporific."[32] In 1925, as radio threatened to cut into reading time, an anthology titled *The Poetry Cure* offered "sedative" poems for "raw and jumpy nerves," "stimulant" poems "to redden pale blood-corpuscles," "tissue builders," "soothers and soporifics," and "accelerators for sluggish blood."[33] Its editor predicted that "when editions of this work begin to dispute front window space in our drug stores, with beauty clays, heating pads, and gland preparations, the market value of the poet will rise."[34] That may not have been just a metaphor: drugstores were one of the first venues for for-profit lending libraries, with the British pharmacy Boots managing to keep one going from 1898 all the way to 1966. Then again, the "gland preparations" that promise to bathe literature in the aura of science can also drag it down to the level of quackery.

Bibliotherapy took on special significance for populations that didn't take access to books for granted. Observing First

World War veterans hospitalized in Tuskegee, the African American librarian Sadie Peterson Delaney concluded that "books, like medicine, have a definite effect on the physical, mental and moral welfare of those who are unfortunately handicapped by illness."[35] The analogy emboldened her to yoke "biblio" with "therapy."

Delaney went on to develop an elaborate system for recommending books to patients stuck in bed with nothing better to do. The bridge that she built between hospitals and libraries became more and more trafficked over the course of the twentieth century. As ledgers, card catalogs, microfiches, and CD-ROMs came and went, occupational therapists and social workers mounted successive campaigns for "bibliopathy," "bibliocounseling," "biblioguidance," and "literatherapy."[36]

Even if you believe that books can improve mood, though, there's no consensus about how. Do books work like a mirror, a painkiller, or a piece of exercise equipment? Some twentieth-century thinkers focused on the connections that readers forge with characters. As James Baldwin put it, "You think your pain and your heartbreak are unprecedented in the history of the world. But then you read."[37] This is a view taken up, too, by contemporary bibliotherapists who promise patients that "our own life mirrored in that of another person" can enable introspection or combat stigma.[38] Hospital nurses have long encouraged the downcast to compare themselves to the patient in the next bed. The patient on the next page, too, can help us feel less alone (if she's just as badly off) or count our blessings (if her wound goes even deeper). A more didactic version of the misery-loves-company justification asked characters to set an example for solving their problems and overcoming their suffering. Yet if fiction serves, as one researcher put it in 1985, to make readers "vicariously experience the surmountable struggles of others," it becomes unclear what we should do with that most literary of endings, an unhappy one.[39]

Twentieth-century bibliotherapists were just as interested in form as in content. Regardless of the behavior represented, they hypothesized, narrative models how to weave disparate events into a continuous identity. At an even higher level of abstraction, some twentieth-century scientists believed that literary patterning could help readers make sense of their own life stories even without taking the form of narrative. The literary critic Meredith Martin has reconstructed one Scottish hospital's attempt to rehabilitate World War I veterans through poetry writing, in the hope that the regularity of the meter would restore the control stripped away by trauma. In Martin's analysis, the cure lay less in the topic or even the act of self-expression than in the shapeliness of the language.[40]

Some twenty-first-century researchers, in contrast, posit that when it comes to mood boosting, neither the content nor the form of literature matters so much as the medium of print. When a study of teenagers finds that "major depressive disorder is positively associated with popular music exposure and negatively associated with reading print media such as books,"[41] or when readers' heart rates and muscle tension are measured to prove books "68% better at reducing stress levels than listening to music,"[42] the researchers don't ask whether the pages contain a bedtime story or a thriller. Likewise, the team of Yale epidemiologists that in 2016 correlated reading with life expectancy weren't distinguishing books about longevity from books about disease. Rather, they plotted the consumption of long-form books against news and magazine reading.[43]

In other words, whereas the history of psychiatry might reflect a shifting focus from the medium (talk therapy, book, or app) to the message, the shift from books as disease carriers to books as cure-alls goes together with a shift from the message to the medium. Nineteenth-century experts worried that readers might imitate novelistic characters who stole or adultered. Twentieth-century thinkers replaced crime with mental health, hoping that fictional plots and forms might model how readers could overcome their inner struggles. Twenty-first-century researchers ratcheted that down—or perhaps up—to the wager that paper and ink, whatever messages they convey, can heal the body and mind.

In that respect, books aren't alone. Reading Well began to surprise me less when I began to notice other objects once associated with pleasure and serendipity being "prescribed." In Britain, GPs began to prescribe exercise in the form of gym vouchers. A diabetic in New York showed me his prescription for vegetables.[44] As books go, so goes food; the fear that consuming too much of the wrong things might endanger the soul gives way to the hope that consuming enough of the right ones might save the body.[45] And if books aren't the only new treatment making their way onto the shelves of virtual pharmacies, conversely doctors' offices aren't the only place where novels are being asked to heal. And like cafes whose turmeric tonics promise benefits to the immune system as well as the taste buds, for-profit ventures have also begun to peddle literature by touting its medical uses.

One sweltering day in 2013, I made my way across London
to the best-known such venture. A high-rent storefront spelling
out School of Life advertising, author talks, singles nights, and
"Conversation Cocktails" led to a front room crammed with
items that old-fashioned bookstores banish to a single rack near
the cash register. Here, on the contrary, a few books punctu-
ated a mob of paperweights, "Emotional Baggage" tote bags,
and candles named after writers (the Walden, incongruously,
smelled like a geranium). The back room, meanwhile, derived
a vaguely Freudian gestalt from its tufted couch. The "bibliotherapists" operating out of the back office, Susan Elderkin and
Ella Berthoud, scribbled a faux prescription pad with recommendations ranging from the allopathic (racing through a nail-
biter like *The Postman Always Rings Twice* heals apathy) to the
analogic (short stories treat diarrhea). You get toothaches, they
explained; so does Count Vronsky.

Ten pounds bought me Elderkin and Berthoud's *The Novel
Cure: An A–Z of Literary Remedies*. I could have paid one hundred for a personalized session, or forty more if "couples' bibliotherapy" had appealed to me and my husband the biography
buff. Each service charged for the kind of recommendations
traditionally given out in bookstores. The difference is that Berthoud and Elderkin weren't actually selling the books.

Some bibliotherapists do. In Bath, the health resort where
Jane Austen characters once flirted with fellow patients whose
doctors had prescribed the thermal waters, one bookstore opened
a "bibliotherapy room," also branded as "reading spa." A Berlin
"book pharmacy" sells beauty products packaged with books
"specially selected for their cleansing, soothing and revitalizing

qualities."[46] Packaging treats as treatment, this version of bibliotherapy has more in common with aromatherapy than with chemotherapy.

While self-help books provide a cheaper alternative to face-to-face treatment, biblioconcierges emerged on the contrary as an upmarket alternative to what librarians have long done for free.[47] And then there are the hidden costs. "Buy *The Enchanted April*," Elderkin and Berthoud's bibliotherapy manual commands, "then book a villa in Tuscany and read it on the way out."[48] If making your own reservation proves too onerous, its authors can chaperone you and your airport novels to a £1,600 oceanfront "bibliotherapy retreat." As bibliotherapists, Elderkin and Berthoud are more like sommeliers than like doctors—or perhaps baristas customizing the literary Frappuccino to every reader's finicky taste.

Yet in doing so, Elderkin and Berthoud forget that reaching for a book is a meaningful act—as transformative, in some cases, as reading it. A service that spares readers the labor of serendipitous fumbling around the stacks means missing out on two advantages that books have over other media—that you can read them for free in the library (at least if you live in a neighborhood that has one), that you can read them in secret (at least if neither a government nor an ebook retailer nor an e-reading platform is tracking you). In the Renaissance, you'll remember from Chapter 1, printed books were among the first mass-produced, mass-marketed objects; in the nineteenth century, they were the first consumer good to be displayed on open-access shelves rather than kept behind the counter. The prescription metaphor thrusts them back into the hands of experts.

Paperback-era English professors promised that reading would impart "transferable skills" (critical thinking, clear writing). Digital-era clinicians promise that literature will heal, or at least will comfort. Auden said that "poetry makes nothing happen." The NHS's claim that literature can heal lends institutional weight to what I'd long felt with more conviction than evidence: that texts *do* make something happen to their readers. What surprised and ultimately dismayed me, though, was the content of that "something." After years of turning to books for stimulus, I had a hard time accepting that they might settle or sedate. In overselling the book's power to calm and console, these therapeutic claims undersell its responsibility to upset and anger us.

Until the turn of the twentieth century, fiction distracted from self-improvement. Novel reading was what clergy, teachers, and doctors were trying to crowd out when they recommended conduct books that spoke directly to the reader in the second person and the imperative mode. Only now, as literature takes on moral and medical powers, self-help books begin to look like the lazy option.

Searching for an adjective to characterize "non-occupational reading," Sven Birkerts comes up with "restorative."[49] A simpler adjective might once have come to mind: call it "pleasure." In 2003, a book-length book list, Nancy Pearl's *Book Lust: Recommended Reading for Every Mood, Moment, and Reason*, anticipated *The Novel Cure*'s pairing of books to moods. As "cure" replaces "lust," reading moved from the bed to the couch. The medicalization of pleasure collapses the distinction that separates Books on Prescription from Mood-Boosting Books.

When Berthoud reshelved fiction under a self-help call number, she chipped away at the centuries-old idea that literature is valuable precisely because it takes us away from our own lives and petty dilemmas.

Book titles are mutating to match. Instead of calling his primer *An Introduction to W. H. Auden*, Alexander McCall Smith has titled it *What W. H. Auden Can Do for You* (2013).[50] *Ten Poems to Change Your Life* (2001) was one-upped nine years later by an anthology of *Poems That Will Save Your Life*. By 2015, American conservative Rod Dreher hedged his bets by shoehorning life-changing *and* lifesaving powers into a single memoir, *How Dante Can Save Your Life: The Life-Changing Wisdom of History's Greatest Poem*.

Back in 1934, Ezra Pound's *ABC of Reading* called literature "news that stays news." An updated definition: news you can use.[51] As the fiction reading that once prompted self-abuse gets reshelved under self-help, so the greedy page-turning that once counted as self-harm becomes another form of self-care. In 2017, *Expecto Patronum: Using the Lessons from Harry Potter to Recover from Abuse* offered lessons from the most-read book in recent history. In 2018, Laura Freeman's memoir, *The Reading Cure*, credited Siegfried Sassoon's descriptions of soft-boiled eggs with curing her anorexia.

The paradox is that essayists who task novel reading or poetry reading with saving or changing their lives wager that we'll spend at least a good portion of our lives reading . . . essays. As Clay Shirky points out, "an entire literature about the value of reading Proust is now more widely read than Proust's actual oeuvre."[52] Every minute that you give to *How Proust Can Change Your Life* is a minute that you're not spending with

Remembrance of Things Past. Yet reading about the experience of reading literature is not the same as reading literature. Even if poetry itself can save your life, Jill Bialosky's prose memoir *Poetry Will Save Your Life* (2017) is unlikely to save yours.

And even if you do read Proust, you may enjoy him less. Panting to find out what happens next, seeing the world through a character's eyes, wallowing in the play of language—all become means to medical ends. In the process, novels may cease to provide an alternative—even a challenge—to the DSM's checkboxes.

To say that books are good for mental health isn't to say that that's all they're good for. But psychologists like Edward L. Deci find that associating extrinsic rewards with an action decreases our sense of its intrinsic value enough to cancel out the effect of those rewards.[53] (The classic example: snacks for blood donors can sap the idealism that motivates volunteers to give platelets for free.) As blueberries marketed for their cancer-fighting flavonoids begin to taste less luscious, reading may lose more prestige than it gains when white-coated experts replace librarians' advice. It's too soon to tell whether the power to heal or at least numb will crowd out all the other reasons for which people have read—to save their souls or to sharpen their wits, to imagine other lives or to better their own. What has already become clear is that there's a price to pay.

After spending as many hours reading Victorian novel haters as interviewing twenty-first-century scientists, I'm left wondering whether to believe the old theories or the new. On mornings when the urge to find out how a story ends is all that gets me out of bed, I think Mood-Boosting Books are on to something. When the telltale compression of pages or the dwindling scroll bar warns me that the imaginative world in which I'm taking refuge is about to come to an end, though, books feel more like intimations of mortality.

For years I rationed Trollope novels, keeping a new one in reserve next to the unopened chocolate bar stashed away for consolation if and when my equally bookish boyfriend walked out. But when I turned the last page of *The Last Chronicle of Barset*, it was Trollope's series that abandoned me. Elderkin and Berthoud are right to dedicate an entry to "finishing, fear of." Whatever life lessons we can glean from having read, perhaps being in the middle of a book is what really counts as living.

Chapter 5

BOUND BY BOOKS

I N 2005, National Public Radio book critic Maureen Corrigan entitled her memoir *Leave Me Alone, I'm Reading*. Corrigan memorializes a mother who warned her against ruining her eyes over a book—every page read an act of rebellion. Sven Birkerts's *Gutenberg Elegies*, too, are fueled by a childhood spent using books to "seal myself off as fully as possible" from a father "with a quick temper and an impatient disdain for anything that smacked of reverie or private absorption, almost as if these states in some way challenged his authority." A third midlife book reviewer, humorist Joe Queenan, structured his 2012 memoir by contrasting his own surreptitious reading of James Bond novels at school with the assignments of teachers who "rammed books down my throat" and the "grumpy, autocratic, middle-aged women who seemed to dislike children" but nonetheless staffed the children's section of his local library. When these readers reach back to remember a childhood that predates digital media, they're also grasping at their own not-yet-professionalized selves, before reading became an activity done for pay and for publication.

In the genre that Mikita Brottman dubs "bibliofessional" (Seth Lerer's alternative coinage is "biblioautobiography"), the narrator's parents must nag him or her to stop reading under the covers, the narrator's spouse must complain that the bookshelves are a health hazard, and the narrator must diagnose herself or himself as a "book addict."[1] Just as rom-coms rarely feature arranged marriages, so autobibliographies—my own term of choice—ignore the parents who set up children with books. "To be literate is to become liberated from the constraints of dependency" declares one expert.[2] In real life, though, toddlers themselves can't buy or borrow their first picture books. In real life, the lobby against library funding cuts is spearheaded by mothers.[3] The myth of the self-made reader airbrushes out the parents who sent the child to school, the teachers who taught them letters, and the other adults who put books in their hands.[4] Yet left-leaning bibliofessors live by Margaret Thatcher's dictum when it comes to reading: there is no such thing as society.

Myths persist because they flatter. By reducing parents, librarians, and teachers to blocking figures, autobibliography emphasizes the reader's quirky pluckiness. Stripped of logistical contingencies, the meeting of a reader's mind with an author's shines out unmediated, unchaperoned. But erasing the middleman sells short one of the book's most powerful capacities: binding readers together.

Even when the hands through which a book has passed belong to an unidentified stranger, its content can gain value from the mere fact that we aren't the first to read it. French anthropologist Michèle Petit observed librarians surreptitiously sneaking books whose circulation they wanted to boost onto the returns cart. They had realized that people were likelier to pick up a book that they thought some other patron had taken the trouble of borrowing—a wordless recommendation.[5]

One way to measure the strength of the bond between library users is to trace the fears inspired by their proximity to one another. When public libraries opened in the middle of the nineteenth century around the English-speaking world, so did debates about whether citizens should share books. At stake were books as much as texts—that is, objects as much as words. The civic spaces established in Britain by the 1850 Public Libraries Act enshrined pages prethumbed by one reader, and soon to be rethumbed by another. But the librarians who agreed that sharing books drew readers together disagreed about whether that was a good thing. In 1890, it was a librarian who invented the "book disinfector" to shield middle-class patrons from the germs of dirtier borrowers. This gas chamber for books, a "metal fumigator made from 16th wire gauge sheet iron, with angle iron door-supports and side-shelf rests," provided a kind of analog virus protection for the trashy novels favored by convalescent girls.[6]

Some Victorians strove to disentangle communication with authors' minds from pages tainted with communicable diseases. At the end of the nineteenth century, best-selling novelist Marie Corelli ranted that "to borrow one's mental fare from Free Libraries is a dirty habit. . . . The true lover of books will never want to peruse volumes that are *thumbed and soiled* by hundreds of other *hands* . . . messy *knockabout volumes*, which many of our medical men assure us carry disease-germs in their too-frequently *fingered* pages."[7] We often speak of ideas poisoning readers' minds. Corelli's fear was different: shared pages, she thought, could literally infect their bodies.

Like public swimming pools, public libraries continued to form a testing ground for hopes and fears about civic connection. As late as 1988, a nurse at a New York hospital who contacted the local branch library to check out books for AIDS patients was turned away: library volunteers refused to handle any books that had passed through HIV-positive readers' hands.[8] Like readers' bodies, books looked like disease carriers. Books that circulated too widely became a stand-in for gay men suspected of dangerous promiscuity. Whose hands you allow to touch the books that you yourself will go on to handle declares whose fellow humanity you recognize.

In the digital era, the transitive property that makes holdable, smearable objects into vectors for disease has become more salient than ever. The difference is that the connections once feared by policy makers are now actively cultivated. When Berlin librarians decided to grant borrowing privileges to undocumented refugees, they made access to books a common ground that cut across divisions of citizenship and language.[9] Access to books, but also to the company of other readers—giving someone the right to handle books that have been, or will be, handled by her neighbors means giving her the right to belong.

At the beginning of this millennium, Deborah Brandt coined the term "sponsors of literacy" to encompass all those people and organizations who "enable, support, teach, and model, as well as recruit, regulate, suppress, or withhold literacy—and gain advantage by it in some way."[10] In conditioning salvation on the ability to read the word of God, the Protestant Reformation gave the faithful not just a reason to be literate, but responsibility for encouraging others' literacy, by any means necessary. Only once public school systems and libraries took over from church-sponsored education did children (and some adults) become a captive audience for secular publishers.

We may be living in the middle of a second such shift. Twenty-first-century required reading is as likely to come from probation officers as from teachers or pastors. And some activist organizations thrust books into potential readers' hands. In the United Kingdom, the Give a Book program donates new books to primary schoolchildren and kids in foster care, as well as to readers who are ill, imprisoned, or old. Others defend marginalized readers by championing persecuted books: one Houston Community College professor's brainchild, Librotraficante, distributes banned books in low-income communities, creating oases in book deserts. And some make bookselling a means to the end of book giving: Better World Books, founded in 2002, sells used books on Amazon to raise funds for literacy-related nonprofits. The doctors whom we met in the previous chapter are only one of several professions that have begun to encourage or even require reading—and not the only ones who do so with government support.

What these organizations encourage is not just reading, but more specifically shared reading. Andrew Piper's 2012 polemic *Book Was There* usefully distinguishes three goals of what he calls "social reading": "commonality" (wanting others to read what we're reading), "transferability" (the right to send that reading material to someone else), and "sociability" (conditions under which we can talk to one another about what we're reading).[11] Sociability doesn't have to take place in libraries: Reach Out and Read, founded in Boston in 1989, gives doctors and pediatric nurses picture books to hand to patients. If waiting rooms can be the scene of reading, so can the tops of dryers. Libraries Without Borders places copies of books in laundromats in the Bronx, the only borough in New York that at the time of writing lacked a single independent bookstore. (In Mott Haven, painters are at work on a crowdfunded bookstore-cum-wine-bar called the Lit. Bar, whose book club has already launched online.)

Then again, we've seen that most reading has always happened outside of libraries, wherever readers have time to kill. A Harlem nonprofit called Barbershop Books builds on that tradition by providing picture books to read aloud while waiting for a haircut. This brainchild of a children's book author reinvents the coif-'n'-read multitasking that one eighteenth-century aristocrat perfected by "reading to two or three others the seventh volume of *Clarissa*, whilst her maid curled her hair, and the poor girl let fall such a shower of tears upon her lady's head, that she was forced to send her out of the room to compose herself."[12] In both cases, reading becomes an element of social life rather than a retreat from it.

Passionate readers are rarely content to read themselves. Most have equally strong feelings about whether and what the people around them should read. And no neat line divides literary nourishment from force-reading. Consider Changing Lives Through Literature, an alternative-sentencing program that gathers convicted offenders together with judges and probation officers to discuss photocopied short stories. It's common enough for probation to be conditioned on attending a twelve-step meeting or a group therapy session, but these readers stay out of jail only as long as they attend biweekly literary discussions. Asked how the book club changed them, participants come up with Christian terms that were borrowed by the midcentury American New Critics: "turning points" and "epiphanies." "When it's working," the program's founder tells me, "this discussion has a kind of magic to it."

The same justice system that requires these men to read or go to jail forbids prisoners from being sent certain books—hardbacks that can be used as weapons; texts that preach violence; books not available through the businesses that have negotiated a monopoly on supplying goods to prisons. Books' danger, in this system, is seen to lie in their physical form as much as in the ideas that they contain. In 2006, Beard v. Banks upheld prisons' right to deny inmates in solitary confinement access to printed matter. Books, the ruling claimed, could be used to fling feces or start fires. In Changing Lives Through Literature, we can glimpse the obverse of that censorship.

It may be too soon to understand how the seepage of reading recommendations from school to NGO will alter the landscape created almost two centuries ago by the handover from church to school. But these organizations recognize what biblio-autobiographies, in casting books as liberators and imagining the library as the one place where otherwise powerless readers can escape all social constraints, obscure. Often, the choice to read comes from above as much as within.

The court-ordered reading group favors stories that prompt empathy and chart transformation. Other NGOs, though, shift emphasis from the adjective "reading" to the noun "group." At the opposite end of London from the high-end bibliotherapy service, I make my way through a door imperfectly scrubbed of graffiti. In the entrance of the senior center, a faded portrait shows a young Queen Elizabeth snipping the building's ribbon. A dozen retirees perch on folding chairs fingering photocopies of the opening chapter of a Somerset Maugham novella, *The Painted Veil*.

Asking what brought each of them to this reading group, I hear story after story of loss. A retired grocery checker uses books to ease herself into sleep, as a long-dead mother once read her bedtime stories. Another retiree describes the garden she used to weed on the weekends she didn't spend hiking with her now-ex-husband. These days, a bad knee converges with a bad divorce to rule out both pleasures—but she still has books.

The circle at the senior center is only one of a few hundred groups organized by Get into Reading, a mushrooming nonprofit that gathers people who are socially marginalized in some way—whether because they're unemployed, imprisoned, ill, or just old—to listen to each other read poems and short stories aloud.

I expected the group to feel cozy. Instead, the room felt raw, exposed. One of the first group meetings fell silent in embarrassment, its organizer told me, when a hitherto unnoticed participant burst into tears midpoem. When the woman took out her purse, her neighbors began fishing for a tissue, but what she wanted turned out to be her wallet. She folded up the photocopy, carefully, to stuff it there for safekeeping.[13]

Most reading groups could more accurately be called "talking groups": when members of a book club gather to discuss what they remember of what they've read, the reading itself has already happened somewhere else, alone. Before coming together with the group, each participant (in theory, at least) has scanned pages in silence, or perhaps listened to an audiobook through noise-isolating earbuds. As classicist Joseph Howley points out, the Greek and Latin terms for "well-read" or "cultured" or "learned"—πεπαιδευμένος *eruditus*—"are perfect passive verbs: we judge someone intelligent now because they have in the past been subjected to good reading."[14] Get into Reading groups, in contrast, emphasize the present tense and real time.

Nothing further from my own college classroom, where the only student who reads in full view is a bad student—the laggard who has failed to do the reading in advance and now must furtively scan the pages that form the backstory of group discussion. The reading group in the senior center may have looked like a classroom, but it sounded like a church—like the hum of a congregation. The nonprofit's founder, a Liverpudlian ex-literary critic named Jane Davis, says that she turned to literature to fill religion's traditional function of "building empathy, shared meaning and social ties: whatever we threw out with the religious bath water."[15] She's quick, though, to counterbalance the analogy of the church with a less goody-goody precedent. What she seeks in reading groups, she explains, is the camaraderie that the working-class neighborhood where she grew up sought in the pub.

Real-time sharing isn't confined to Get into Reading. Like the members of yeshivas, madrassas, and monasteries, participants in secular reading groups are beginning to read in concert rather than discuss what they remember of what they read. These groups don't even need to involve voicing the text. US-based "silent book clubs" are fueled by the insight that in a life where overscheduling makes it hard to carve out time to sit tête-à-tête with a book, scheduling a grown-up version of study hall in the same café or park or bar where others are reading their own (different) books can be a way to connect at once to books and to other readers: the literary equivalent of a headphone party.[16] Perhaps books can fence and bridge at the same time—can help us be, in the resonant words of sociologist Sherry Turkle, "alone together."[17]

However different their methods, cognitive and social scientists agree in looking for empathy at the level of literary representation: their studies gauge how intensely readers imagine the thoughts and feelings of literary characters. The community organizers whom I met, though, were as interested in objects as in words. Where texts allow us to camp out in characters' heads, these organizers realized that books can nudge us to picture other eyes scanning the same page, and other hands holding the same volume.

Get into Reading could easily be mistaken for a more socially inclusive variant of the bibliotherapy we encountered in the previous chapter. Funded in part by NHS grants, its reading groups do indeed tackle mental-health problems like isolation, stigma, and even depression. But where a bibliotherapist might ask participants to read texts about loneliness or find solace merely in the medium of print, Get into Reading gambles that both the subject of the text and its medium are beside the point.

I thought back to the Toni Morrison character who feared touching the same Bible that had been touched by her African American servant. Where texts train readers to empathize with fictional characters, books allow readers to bond with each other. Where Books on Prescription makes self-help volumes a substitute for face-to-face encounters with a mental health provider, the community organizers I met make reading an excuse for social interaction. Where bibliotherapists work to help the individual patient or the individual consumer, these organizers—call them biblioactivists—use books to forge community. And where beachfront reading retreats protect bibliotherapy clients from the masses huddled in the public library, social justice campaigners deploy the love of books to cut across social divisions.

Some biblioboosters are rich or famous. Since 1995 the Parton-funded Dollywood Foundation, based in Sevier County, Tennessee, has been one of the United States' largest purchasers of children's books, which it gives away to children up to the age of five. But books can also be weapons of the weak. Some bibliovolunteers lack the money to collect precious volumes or even to own a bookcase.

I met one such activist in a London church's parking lot. Wedged between two smart cars was a dented white van whose plywood shelves buckled under the pressure of an Arabic Bible, odd numbers of a magazine called *Tunnels and Tunneling*, and duplicates of an advertisement-stuffed directory of Polish business in Britain, now three years out of date.[18] The van's sponsor, Quaker Homeless Action, helps readers who are sleeping rough reclaim a right that many citizens take for granted: book borrowing.

One of the few male volunteers ducks out of the van's cramped doorway with the help of a cane like the one that mortarboarded schoolmasters hit him with at a high-end grammar school many decades ago, "like Wackford Squeers," the whack-happy villain of a Dickens novel that he read to death half a century ago, he explains. But he doesn't own the copy on which he spilled tea in those days, or any other book from before 2005, when he was evicted following a bad breakup.

He found his way to the bookmobile a few years later, set on the trail by an acquaintance who had been carting around an exhibition catalog nestled in torn bubble wrap: a coffee table book without a coffee table. Agatha Christie and Karl May filled the hours when the shelter was closed: 6 a.m. to 10 p.m. is a rather long time to get through. Plastic bags formed make-shift tarps for the few books that made their way into the cart that held his own possessions. As soon as he found housing again, he volunteered.

Like every library, this one is defined as much by what it excludes as by what it stocks. Its volunteers reject Marie Kondo fans' purged DIY guides, picture books, romance novels, and travel books. Hardbacks, decorative objects as well as reading material for the housed, are usually at the bottom of homeless readers' wish list. If you own no desk or even toilet top, cloth-bound volumes begin to look like a grotesque design failure: heavy to hoist onto your back, cumbersome to cram in a repurposed shopping cart, more vulnerable than even a person is to the lightest rain shower. Project Gutenberg downloads, in contrast, don't load you down, and old-model smartphones without a SIM card can be found for cheap. A built-in light source aids more than reading: the medium of enlightenment doubles as a flashlight.

The van admits all readers. In that respect, it's unusual. Long before internet filters, one Victorian librarian inked out the betting news in every newspaper in order to block out "numbers of rough and ill-behaved fellows, who . . . persisted in disturbing the peace of the reading rooms, and interfering with the comfort of quiet readers."[19] In 1920, one Birmingham librarian complained that "no delicacy seemed to deter the poor tramp from using, not only the news-room, but the best seats in the reference library for a snooze."[20] And battles over whether to exclude some from library borrowing—or even library entering—in the nineteenth century are not over yet. Some librarians continue to insist that "a library is not a refuge for the homeless." A double standard masks the fact that middle-class readers, too, have bodies. As one defender of class-blind access points out, those same librarians would never exclude "toddlers, who can be smelly and loud, are not . . . reading anything and are often asleep."[21]

Even the growing consensus among librarians that everyone should be able to enter the reading room rarely translates into enabling homeless men and women to borrow. Life on the street lacks the predictability of a four-week loan period. Books get wet, get lost, get stolen (usually by someone disappointed to discover that the bag he's snagged contains nothing more usable than printed pages). Networks formal and informal respond to that problem: day centers improvise a shelf or two where books can be taken and left; readers alert one another to the curbs across which evicted textbooks sprawl every June.

By taking books to readers rather than waiting for readers to come to books, the London bookmobile courts the very promiscuity Victorian book disinfectors attempted to ward off. In both cases, the medium is part of the message. Yet if the bookmobile asserts the value of community, it also enshrines autonomy. Unlike the probation officers taking attendance at the court-ordered reading group, the bookmobile's volunteers don't monitor reading or talking. Unlike World Book Day's subway distributors, they don't dictate what books get read. Unlike the doctors who prescribe books, they don't prejudge what moods or behaviors should result from reading. No gossip about literary characters, no turn taking, no unison, no end to which reading is simply a means. Where Jane Davis enlists reading to combat isolation, the bookmobile defends individuals' right to choose what to read and how to talk about it. More: whether to talk at all.

Nothing incendiary about the words of a Spanish martial-arts manual that lies on the bookmobile shelf next to a Lithuanian translation of Alexander McCall Smith. The white van's political power lies elsewhere. If the meaning of books resides not just in the texts they contain but in the paths that they take to reach a reader, then it may matter less whether a book makes an argument about community than whether it's bought with a click and delivered by a drone, recommended by a familiar neighborhood bookseller, or handed over for free by a volunteer who lingers to discuss it.

Writing texts or designing books, therefore, aren't the only outlets for booklovers' creativity. Like World Book Night's creators, the activists who launched the bookmobile invest equal ingenuity in fashioning distribution systems. And if we take "activism" to encompass not just the content of texts but the channels through which they flow, then biblioactivists can be publishers, librarians, even booksellers.

No longer just sellers and buyers, independent booksellers and their customers have come to see themselves as engaging in a political act. Just as in an age of agribusiness Prince Charles could reinvent himself as an organic farmer, so the age of the deep-discounting online retailer has witnessed the emergence of the gentlewoman bookseller. The past decade has seen a spate of celebrities bailing out, buying, and discreetly subsidizing local bookstores—not just authors like Judy Blume and Ann Patchett but also Google cofounder Sergey Brin, a Robin Hood recycling digital profits into wood-pulp subventions.[22] What they're rescuing isn't just books, but also the human beings who vend and recommend them. The bookseller becomes an endangered species, as worthy of saving as a wetland or a whale.

More radical, though, are those publishers and distributors who invent ways to bypass the market. In Thoreau's hometown, the Free Press requires anyone who wants one of its books to donate to charity whatever they judge the book is worth—a triangular payment rather than a one-to-one exchange. The press asks recipients to pass the book along to someone else when they're done; like many software publishers, this publisher doesn't offer an object to keep so much as a limited-time experience. The texts chosen engage slyly with economic questions: a volume of essays about money, a novel featuring a jewel thief.[23] Authors donate their time too. That may be less of an innovation; the wife of one contributor described the Free Press as "a new way for writers to not make money."[24]

In Barcelona in 2015, a few friends began soliciting donations of books to hand out—with a catch. Their project, 1010 Ways to Buy Books Without Money, bartered books for actions. You could earn one book by giving blood, earn another by smiling at a neighbor, gain access to a third by promising to perform oral sex on your partner. Mixing archness with earnestness, a fourth volume was offered in exchange for a signed promise to quit smoking.

These triangular payments set books apart from other commodities, declaring them too sacred to be bought and sold. In the process, books are analogized to other substances that stand above the market. As ethics rules bar blood donors from taking payment for their platelets, so the Free Press's refusal to charge brackets books with human organs, sex, and love.

That printed books are the granddaddy of all commodities may make it seem unprecedented how vehemently these book-lovers oppose buying and selling them. We've seen books pioneer self-service retailing in the eighteenth century, consumer credit in the nineteenth, automated inventory control in the twentieth, and e-commerce in the twenty-first. Compared to those innovations in marketing and distributing, biblioactivists' search for alternatives to the cash nexus could be lumped with Amtrak's "library atmosphere" as one more instance of digital dwellers idealizing the special occasions on which they visit the world of print.[25]

Yet even if placing books on a pedestal untainted by commerce breaks with their long history as its spearhead, circulating books through ad hoc networks of readers continues the even longer history that we've witnessed of books being gifted, lent, shared, and read aloud. The Free Press can be seen as face-to-face successors to crowdsourced enterprises like Project Gutenberg, which attempted to free books from the market by digitizing the words that print originally vehicled. Decades before ebooks came to mean in-copyright words purveyed by a for-profit corporation, Project Gutenberg's dozens and then hundreds of volunteers disseminated the books they loved not by standing on street corners, but by proofreading digital files recognizable by the almost Protestant austerity of ASCII files with raggedy margins.[26] They loved books enough to donate their time and eyesight to make it available outside of the market, and loved the democratizing potential of the nascent internet enough to do that through exchanges with strangers whom they'd never meet, rather than through a local library or book club.

Later, nonprofit book digitization projects undertaken by the Internet Archive and HathiTrust would continue to avoid the licensing restrictions imposed by for-profit corporations such as Amazon. Because print isn't the only medium in which texts can be distributed outside of the market, biblioactivism cuts across any neat line separating print from digital reading. The volunteers who give away printed books, and digital information about printed books, mimic the circulation of electronic shareware—software whose mode of distribution is designed to boost community rather than bottom lines.

Although English professors number among those volunteers, biblioactivists are likelier to perceive us the way Joe Queenan perceived the grumpy librarians of his childhood. Whether addressing the residents of a blighted housing project or servicing the worried well-heeled, whether trained in social work or in marketing, the biblioactivists I met, too, described their role in a populist language that maintained a wary distance from English departments. Each one claimed to speak for common sense and common readers. Each endeavored to wrest great books away from jargon-loving literary-critical killjoys whose chaperoning interrupts literature lovers' heavy petting.

If literature cultivates empathy, I ask Jane Davis, the founder of Get into Reading, why do I leave every English department meeting wanting to strangle my colleagues? She asks, in return, whether I've heard of molecular gastronomy. By asking what we can learn about texts rather than *from* texts, by striving for originality at the expense of common sense, we're cooking up the intellectual equivalent of the outlandish dishes invented by celebrity chefs. What you and your colleagues write, she tells me, is snail-flavored porridge.[27]

Davis's stomach-churning metaphor made me worry that attempts to open literature up might wall literary criticism off. Cultural studies once offered nonacademic readers tools with which to critique nonliterary objects, such as advertising or political oratory or other forms of propaganda. But as academics' crit without lit has given way to biblioactivists' lit without crit, university English departments relinquished their role—forged during the Cold War—of providing a training ground for method that could later be applied to public and private propaganda. Biblioactivists, in contrast, wager that the civic engagement that books can teach consists of . . . distributing more books.

We love and hate characters, but we also love and hate other readers. Although the English language has a word for eating together ("commensality," in case you were wondering), I've searched dictionaries in vain to find a name for readers' parallel play—for the reading that happens in subways and churches as much as in libraries and classrooms. Or in beds: my husband and I didn't really feel the weight of our vows until, unloading volumes from one final U-Haul, we started to interfile.

But loving books doesn't necessarily mean loving other people who love books for a different reason, or put them to a different use. Like Gideons, English professors spend their lives trying to thrust the books that they value the most into other people's hands. Also like Gideons, though, English professors spend our time trying to break other people's habits. Every time I met a doctor who prescribed books or a volunteer who drove a bookmobile or a dog lover who trained poodles to listen to children read aloud, I saw myself in a distorted mirror. Literary critics themselves have sometimes contrasted academic reading to pleasure reading, imagined as a spontaneous, individual welling-up of desire rather than as a set of learned practices. We might learn from biblioactivists that pleasure, like misery, needs company.

English professors nag our students to resist the temptation to skip and skim, we wheedle them to care enough to finish the reading. But beyond influencing whether our students read, we also determine (or try to determine) how. We coax freshmen to care *less* about the world represented in fiction, shaming those who read for the plot or pick favorites among characters. We train them to see past the ostensible subject of a text to its linguistic structures, just as they see past the look and feel of a book to its textual content.[28]

The biblioactivists whom I met eschewed any such critical distance. They struggled, on the contrary, to nudge readers closer to the characters. From them I learned that identifying with the characters wasn't some sloppiness to be slapped down, like splitting infinitives. From their extracurricular reading, I learned that the love of books takes as many different forms as romantic love does—and that the same act that gives pleasure to one person can pain another.

What I've learned from unprofessional booklovers isn't just academic. Like their autobibliographies, mine is a love story entangled with stories of education, conversion, deprogramming. Drawing a salary hasn't stopped me from being a close reader, or a bad reader, or a greedy one. Just as ebooks and print books continue to exist side by side, a reader's middle-aged identities don't displace her childish ones. I read to find company, to cushion heartbreak, to whet desire, to slake curiosity. And I read not just to fumble my way toward what writers have thought and felt, but to piece together the thoughts and feelings of earlier readers.

As leery as I am of making reading a means to the ends of health or empathy or community, as often as I've thought "with friends like this, books don't need enemies"—no matter what, long-form print has remained my own Ritalin and Valium. Like most lovers, I'd rather be the first one to go.

END PAPERS

INCREASINGLY, people of the book are also people of the cloud. At the Codex Hackathon, a convention whose participants spend a frenetic weekend designing electronic reading tools, I watch developers line up onstage to pitch book-related projects to potential collaborators and funders. "Uber for books": a same-day service that would deliver library volumes to your door. "Fitbit for books": an app that blocks incoming calls and buzzes your phone with reminders to get back to a book.[1] That literary pedometer meets its real-world counterpart in LitCity: "Imagine walking down a city street and feeling that familiar buzz of a push notification. But instead of it being a notification on Twitter or a restaurant recommendation, it's a beautiful passage from a work of literature with a tie to that place."[2] I thought back to the nineteenth-century guidebooks that inserted a snippet of Shelley next to their map of the Alps; the book has always been about bringing worlds together.

Some projects return to the decades-old premise of electronic enhancements or "enrichments," which went during the aughts under the ungainly name of "vooks." SubText overlays digitized works of literature with annotations and images; BookPlaylist synchronizes a text with background music. Then again, perhaps print books aren't the ones whose poverty needs to be remedied: other projects feel like pale electronic imitations of features that print books have long taken for granted. Rebook generates digital "association copies" (remember Obama swearing in on Lincoln's Bible) by allowing readers to give away ebooks that they've underlined or annotated. Cover Design History catalogs the dust jackets too often lost when books are digitized or even just discarded by libraries, while Gavel (as in, "you can't judge a book by . . .") uses snapshots of book covers to generate and summarize reviews.

One of the problems being solved is death. Would a diagnosis of terminal cancer be softened by an app that helps you divvy up your books among your heirs? The book may not be dying, but its users seem sensitive to their own mortality. *Fahrenheit 451* ends with characters rescuing books from a biblioclastic regime by choosing a book to "become." You can take a love of reading to mean preserving a threatened past; you can also understand it as a spur to imagining what new forms books might take in the future.

This book opened with Coover's 1992 magazine article "The End of Books," which launched a thousand eulogies for the book as we knew it. Coover took "book" to mean a gathering of printed pages mass-produced on spec to be sold to anonymous strangers in exchange for hard cash. His assumption, we can see now, would have surprised a Victorian circulating-library patron or an eighteenth-century subscriber to a hand-circulated newssheet. But Coover's understanding of what a book is and what a book does would have been equally hard-pressed to include the Free Press's wares.

In 1992, hyperlinks were the killer app. Coover's title punned on the page-turning powers of the codex, which sweeps novel readers inexorably from Page 1 to The End. (The codex replaced the scroll, millennia before Bible.com, precisely because it allowed early Christians to flip hyperactively through their scriptures.) Yet chronology makes it hard to believe that the hyperlink was killing the book, because that metaphor predates the web. In 1835, Théophile Gautier's novel *Mademoiselle de Maupin* declared that "the newspaper is killing the book, as the book killed architecture." Gautier was one-upping Victor Hugo's *The Hunchback of Notre-Dame* (1831), which depicted an archdeacon worrying that the book would kill the cathedral and a bookseller complaining that newfangled printing presses were killing scribes' trade. This nineteenth-century historical novel is set a quarter century after Gutenberg's first Bible, when a thriving industry of manuscript-on-demand was forced to readjust.

In hindsight, we can see how rarely one technology supersedes another: the rise of the podcast makes clear that video didn't doom audio any more than radio ended reading. Yet in 1913, a journalist interviewing Thomas Edison on the future of motion pictures recounted the inventor declaring confidently that "books . . . will soon be obsolete in the public schools."[3] By 1927 a librarian could observe that "pessimistic defenders of the book . . . are wont to contrast the actual process of reading with the lazy and passive contemplation of the screen or listening to wireless, and to prophecy the death of the book." And in

1966, Marshall McLuhan stuck books into a list of outdated antiques: "clotheslines, seams in stockings, books and jobs—all are obsolete."[4]

Throughout the nineteenth century and again in the twentieth, every generation rewrote the book's epitaph. All that changes is whodunnit. Gautier's culprit was a very real historical phenomenon: the daily papers emerging in 1835 thanks to broader literacy, the metal press invented around 1800, and steam printing shortly thereafter. Later sci-fi writers imagined a succession of replacements: "fonografic" recordings (*Library Journal*, 1883), "telephonic sermons" (Edward Bellamy, 1887), VCR-like "Babble Machines" (H. G. Wells, 1899), microfilm-esque "reading-machine bobbins" (Aldous Huxley, 1932), and "spools which projected books" (Ray Bradbury, 1948). In 1885, French librarian R. Balmer gave the names of "whispering-machine" and "metal automatic book" to something that sounds uncannily like an audiobook. Its user "would place the machine in the hat, and have the sounds conveyed to the ear by wires." Besides curing eyestrain, these "reading machines" would "permit of the pursuit simultaneously of physical and of mental improvement." Translation: instead of hunching over desks, intellectuals would be free to jog. And with both hands free, their wives could read while dishwashing: "The problem of the higher education of woman would be triumphantly solved."[5]

The more spandex jumpsuits, the fewer leather-bound volumes: the future was recognizable by its bookshelf-bare walls. The Enlightenment visionary Louis-Sébastien Mercier predicted that in the year 2440, the sprawling bookstacks of the Royal Library would have been condensed into a single volume.

Like a chemist distilling botanical essences, Mercier explained, the editors of the future would "extract the substance of thousands of volumes, which they have included in a small duodecimo"—scaled somewhere between an iPod and an iPad.

History proved Mercier right in one sense: the future lay not with expanding information, but compacting it. By 1961, the Polish fantasist Stanislaw Lem pictured bookshelves squeezed onto what we would now call an e-reader, supplemented by what we would now call print on demand.

> All my purchases fitted into one pocket, though there must have been almost three hundred titles. . . . They can be read with the aid of an opton, which was similar to a book but had only one page between the covers. At a touch, successive pages of the text appeared on it. . . . As a rule, a bookstore had only single "copies" of books, and when someone needed a particular book, the contents of the work was recorded in a crystal. The originals—Crystomatrices—were not to be seen; they were kept behind pale blue enamel steel plates. So a book was printed, as it were, every time someone needed it.[6]

Four years later, Frank Herbert's doorstop-sized *Dune* conjured up a "Bible made for space travelers. Not a filmbook, but actually printed on filament paper." Herbert measured the book, like thumb drives and PalmPilots, against a human body: thanks to a "magnifier and electrostatic charge system," the unabridged volume would take up less space than the joint of your finger.

The term "ebook" endorses such optimism. Whatever replaces the codex, it implies, will be functionally equivalent: the same textual content in a new and improved (usually shrunken) package. A darker strain of futurology, in contrast, emphasizes political decline over technological progress. *Fahrenheit 451* represents book burning as an end in itself, not just a means to suppressing sedition whose medium happens to be print. A few years earlier, *1984* opened with the purchase of a "thick, quarto-sized blank book with a red back and a marbled cover." A blank notebook speaks louder than a printed volume: "Even with nothing written in it, it was a compromising possession." The final piece of evidence of thoughtcrime that sends Winston Smith to Room 101? A paperweight found in his possession. Here as in Amtrak's Quiet Car, the idea of the book remains more powerful than any ideas that it contains.

Fiction has been better at predicting the invention of cylinder books and filament books, or the survival of marbled pages and glass paperweights, than at imaging what as-yet-unborn institutions might in the future carve out room to read. Even the writers whose imaginations run riot in picturing new machines for viewing and storing text either give no space to libraries, bookstores, and postal systems, or imagine those intermediaries as mirror images of their own era. On the eve of World War I, one humorist imagined a day in the life of a late-twentieth-century household:

> There was a knock at the front door, and the young people slid up the moving stairway, anticipating the parcel of books delivered each morning by the public library aeroplane service. They returned disconsolate; it was only the sterilized milk. "You youngsters don't know what hardships are," said the elderly uncle; "when I was a lad, back in 1913, I used to get up at

nine o'clock in the morning and walk the length of the street to get a book from a Carnegie Library."[7]

The librarian fed up with "the death of the book" in 1927 predicts more darkly that in the future "we shall press a button, or turn a handle, and receive the books selected by ourselves— or much more probably by some paternal committee."[8] In the decade when Orwell's dystopia is set, the pulp magazine *Planet Stories* ran Ray Bradbury's second most famous book-burning fable, *Pillar of Fire*. Washed up in the twenty-fourth century, its time traveler heads straight for the library. For even in a society that torches horror fiction, circulation desks still exist, and their attendants still ask "May I help you?"

> "I'd like to 'have' Edgar Allan Poe." His verb was carefully chosen. He didn't say "read." He was too afraid that books were passé, that printing itself was a lost art. Maybe all "books" today were in the form of fully delineated three-dimensional motion pictures.[9]

However the terms change, fiction makes the place where books are read, had, or received a comforting constant.

Not so in real life. If you believe that infrastructures have consistently done more to shape reading than have this or that device, then the question becomes not whether we read in print or online or in some as-yet-unimagined medium but rather in the interactions through which we get our hands on books— and even more fundamentally, the interactions that awaken a desire for them. Writers who foresaw space travel, time travel, and virtual reality still failed to imagine that libraries that provide more digital and print service than ever before might nonetheless find their staffs fired and replaced by volunteers; their survival dependent on self-help books prescribed by doctors; their Carnegie-era premises sold off to for-profit companies that turn their vaulted reading rooms into private gyms where books are ingested, if at all, through earphones on the treadmill. Whatever its medium, I'm confident that the experience of immersion in a world made of words will survive if and only if readers continue to carve out places and times to have words with one another. As for the marbled notebooks, they can take their chances.

ACKNOWLEDGMENTS

This book owes whatever good it contains to the many librarians, scholars, activists, and other booklovers who took the time away from reading to educate me. In the course of writing it, I racked up particular debts to Ellis Avery, Alida Becker, Doug Beube, Laura Farwell Blake, John Bullock, Katie Calvert, Christopher Cannon, Amanda Claybaugh, Margaret Cohen, Patricia Crain, Jane Davis, Pamela Druckerman, Elizabeth Denlinger, Brian Dettmer, James English, Lynn Festa, Elaine Freedgood, Natalka Freeland, Gary Frost, Lisa Gitelman, Anthony Grafton, Stephen Greenblatt, Mindy Greenstein, Susan Halpert, Odile Harter, David Henkin, Lara Heimert, Isabel Hofmeyr, Jimmie Holland, Madeline Holland, Tom Hyry, Alex Jacobs, Maya Jasanoff, Amanda Katz, Eve Kennedy-Spaien, Thomas Keymer, Matt Kirschenbaum, Katie Lambright, Natasha Barajas Lasky, Michele Lamont, Yoon Sun Lee, Spencer Lenfield, Heather Love, Tina Lupton, Deidre Lynch, Alison MacKeen, Paula McDowell, Meredith McGill, Mark McGurl, Tess McNulty, Sharon Marcus, Tom Mole, Sina Najafi, Geoffrey Nunberg,

Richard Ovenden, Andrew Piper, John Plotz, Jessica Pressman, Richard Price, Sally Price, Simon Reader, Catherine Robson, Hannah Rosefield, Matthew Rubery, Phillipa Rubins, Dana Sajdi, Sharmila Sen, Jan Schramm, Jenny Schuessler, Peter Stallybrass, Ramie Targoff, Pamela Thurschwell, Katie Trumpener, Sezen Unluonen, Susan VanHecke, Jim Wald, Rebecca Walkowitz, Robert Waxler, Porter White, and as always to colleagues at Widener Library, Cambridge Public Library, and to generous strangers on SHARP-L. Thanks, too, to the Guggenheim Foundation and the National Endowment for the Humanities.

Teaching with Ann Blair and with Jill Lepore has given me more than book learning. Maia Silber, extraordinary research assistant turned even more extraordinary historian in her own right, will recognize her work in every word. Nir and Esau: we are in a book.

NOTES

Introduction

1. Sven Birkerts, *The Gutenberg Elegies: The Fate of Reading in an Electronic Age* (Winchester, England: Faber and Faber, 1994).

2. National Endowment for the Arts, *Reading at Risk: A Survey of Literary Reading in America*, 2004, https://arts.gov/sites/default/files/ReadingAtRisk.pdf, and *To Read or Not to Read: A Question of National Consequence*, 2007, http://arts.gov/research/ToRead.pdf.

3. Nicholas Carr, "Is Google Making Us Stupid? What the Internet Is Doing to Our Brains," *Atlantic*, July/August 2008, www.theatlantic.com/magazine/archive/2008/07/is-google-making-us-stupid/6868/.

4. Markus Dohle, "Frankfurt Book Fair 2017: Penguin Random House CEO Markus Dohle's Full Remarks," *Publishers Weekly*, October 15, 2017, www.publishersweekly.com/pw/by-topic/international/Frankfurt-Book-Fair/article/75092-frankfurt-book-fair-2017-penguin-random-house-ceo-markus-dohle-s-full-remarks.html; "Book Publisher Revenue Up for Adult Books, University Presses in 2017," Association of American Publishers, May 9, 2018, http://newsroom.publishers.org/book-publisher-revenue-up-for-adult-books-university-presses-in-2017.

5. Michael Hiltzik, "No, Ebooks Aren't Dying—But Their Quest to Dominate the Reading World Has Hit a Speed Bump," *Los Angeles Times*, May 1, 2017, www.latimes.com/business/hiltzik/la-fi-hiltzik-ebooks-20170501-story.html.

6. Andrew Perrin, "Book Reading 2016," Pew Research Center, September 1, 2016, www.pewinternetinternet.org/2016/09/01/book-reading-2016/.

7. "Book Publishing Annual StatShot Survey Reveals Religious Crossover and Inspirational Books Supported Trade Book Growth in 2016," Association of American Publishers, August 1, 2017, http://news room.publishers.org/book-publishing-annual-statshot-survey-reveals-religious-crossover-and-inspirational-books-supported-tradebook-growth-in-2016/.

8. Ibid.; "Book Formats in the U.S.—Statistics & Facts," Statista, 2018, www.statista.com/topics/3938/book-formats-in-the-us/.

9. "Book Publisher Revenue Up for Adult Books, University Presses in 2017," Association of American Publishers, May 9, 2018, http://news room.publishers.org/book-publisher-revenue-up-for-adult-books-university-presses-in-2017.

10. Alexandra Alter, "Bottleneck at Printers Has Derailed Some Holiday Book Sales," *New York Times*, December 23, 2018, www.nytimes.com/2018/12/23/books/paper-printers-holiday-sales-books-publishers.html.

11. In the United States, book sales have declined from a height of $17.17 billion in 2007 to $10.73 billion in 2017: see "Book Store Sales in the United States from 1992 to 2017 (in Billion U.S. Dollars)," Statista, February 2018, www.statista.com/statistics/197710/annual-book-store-sales-in-the-us-since-1992/. Revenues have dropped over the same period: see "Revenue of Bookstores (NAICS 45121) in the United States from 2010 to 2018 (in Billion U.S. Dollars)," Statista, November 2018, www.statista.com/statistics/249023/bookstore-industry-revenue-in-the-us/. In the United Kingdom, 259 bookstores have closed since 2008: see "Number of Specialized Stores for the Retail Sale of Books in the United Kingdom (UK) from 2008 to 2016," Statista, May 2018, www.statista.com/statistics/295868/book-selling-books-in-specialised-stores-in-the-uk/.

12. Andrew Perrin, "Nearly One-in-Five Americans Now Listen to Audiobooks," Pew Research Center, March 8, 2018, www.pewresearch .org/fact-tank/2018/03/08/nearly-one-in-five-americans-now-listen-to -audiobooks/.

13. Scholastic, Inc., and YouGov, *Kids and Family Reading Report*, 6th ed., 2016, www.scholastic.com/readingreport/files/Scholastic -KFRR-6ed-2017.pdf.

14. Abigail Geiger, "Millennials Are the Most Likely Generation of Americans to Use Public Libraries," Pew Research Center, June 21, 2017, www.pewresearch.org/fact-tank/2017/06/21/millennials-are-the-most -likely-generation-of-americans-to-use-public-libraries/.

15. Brian Mead and Terra Dankowski, "The Library of Things," *American Libraries*, June 1, 2017, https://americanlibrariesmagazine.org/2017 /06/01/library-of-things/; Kristen Arnett, "An Incomplete List of the Non-Book Things You Can Get at the Library," Literary Hub, December 5, 2018, https://lithub.com/an-incomplete-list-of-the-non-book-things -you-can-get-at-the-library/.

16. Susan Orlean, *The Library Book* (New York: Simon & Schuster, 2018), 65.

17. Eric Klinenberg, *Palaces for the People: How Social Infrastructure Can Help Fight Inequality, Polarization, and the Decline of Civic Life* (New York: Crown/Archetype, 2018).

18. Joe Verghese et al., "Leisure Activities and the Risk of Dementia in the Elderly," *New England Journal of Medicine* 348, no. 25 (2003): 2508–2516.

19. "Book Reading," Humanities Indicators, May 2015, https:// humanitiesindicators.org/content/indicatordoc.aspx?i=92.

20. David C. Kidd and Emanuele Castano, "Reading Literary Fiction Improves Theory of Mind," *Science* 342, no. 6156 (2013): 377–380.

21. Gregory S. Berns, Kristina Blaine, Michael J. Prietula, and Brandon E. Pye, "Short- and Long-Term Effects of a Novel on Connectivity in the Brain," *Brain Connectivity* 3, no. 6 (2013): 590–600; Diana I. Tamir, Andrew Bricker, David Dodell-Feder, and Jason P. Mitchell, "Reading Fiction and Reading Minds: The Role of Simulation in the

Default Network," *Social Cognitive and Affective Neuroscience* 11, no. 2 (2015): 215–224.

22. Kathleen Capriotti and Kelly Hill, "Social Effects of Culture: Detailed Statistical Models," *Statistical Insights on the Arts*, Hill Strategies Research Inc., 7, no. 1 (2008): 2.

23. Christina Clark and George Dugdale, *Literacy Changes Lives: An Advocacy Resource* (National Literacy Trust, 2008).

24. Wim Knulst and Gerbert Kraaykamp, "Trends in Leisure Reading: Forty Years of Research on Reading in the Netherlands," *Poetics* 26 (1998): 21–41.

25. Alberto Manguel, *Packing My Library: An Elegy and Ten Digressions* (New Haven, CT: Yale University Press, 2018), 7.

26. On early twentieth-century duplicating technologies, see Robert C. Binkley, "New Tools for Men of Letters," *Yale Review* (1935): 519–537. Thanks to Lisa Gitelman for the reference.

27. For a trenchant critique of this claim, however, see Elyse Graham, *The Republic of Games: Textual Culture Between Old Books and New Media* (Montreal: McGill-Queen's University Press, 2018).

Chapter 1: Reading over Shoulders

1. Tim Harford, "How Ikea's Billy Bookcase Took Over the World," BBC, February 27, 2017, www.bbc.com/news/business-38747485.

2. S. D. Chrostowska, "Shelf Lives: On Nostalgic Libraries," *Public Culture* 28, no. 1, January 2016: 9–21.

3. Nicole Carter, "'Sex and the City' Gets Wed at a Famed Public Library," *New York Daily News*, November 3, 2007, www.nydailynews .com/entertainment/tv-movies/sex-city-wed-famed-public-library -article-1.255256; Doree Shafrir, "Yours for a Day: Eight Fantasy Venues Paired with Reasonable—but Equally Desirable—Alternatives," *New York*, Winter 2010, http://nymag.com/weddings/reception/2010 /winter/venues/.

4. "Consumer Attitudes Towards Books and E-books in the United States as of April 2017," Statista, April 12, 2017, www.statista.com/statistics /707142/attitude-books-e-books/.

5. See Jessica Pressman, "The Aesthetic of Bookishness in Twenty-First-Century Literature," *Michigan Quarterly Review* 48, no. 4, Fall 2009.

6. R. K. Webb, *The British Working Class Reader, 1790–1848: Literacy and Social Tension* (London: Allen & Unwin, 1955), 306. Thanks to Lisa Gitelman for the reference.

7. Kristina Myrvold, *Inside the Guru's Gate: Ritual Uses of Texts Among the Sikhs in Varanasi* (Lund, 2007).

8. For a witty critique of twenty-first-century idealization of reading, see Mikita Brottman, *The Solitary Vice: Against Reading* (Berkeley, CA: Counterpoint, 2008), and "The Reading Crisis," *n+1* 3, Fall 2005; for the longer history of celebrations of print, see Elizabeth L. Eisenstein, *Divine Art, Infernal Machine: The Reception of Printing in the West from First Impressions to the Sense of an Ending* (Philadelphia: University of Pennsylvania Press, 2011).

9. Jo Piazza, "Can Instagram Keep People Reading Books?", *Forbes*, May 25, 2017, www.forbes.com/sites/jopiazza/2017/05/25/instagram-book stagrammers-selling-books/#2e6ea9d1727b.

10. Emma Kantor, "Harnessing Bookstagram: A PAMA Panel," *Publishers Weekly*, May 16, 2017, www.publishersweekly.com/pw/by-topic/childrens /childrens-book-news/article/73612-harnessing-bookstagram-a-pama -panel.html.

11. Danielle Braff, "Millennial, Book and Candle," *New York Times*, January 11, 2019, www.nytimes.com/2019/01/11/style/book-candles.html.

12. Ray Bradbury, "Exchange," *Quicker Than the Eye* (New York: Avon, 1996), 207–219.

13. Brett Spencer, "From Atomic Shelters to Arms Control" *Information and Culture* 49, no. 3 (2014): 351–385.

14. C. Max Magee, "Insidious Devices: An Introduction to 'The Late American Novel,'" *The Millions*, March 1, 2011, https://themillions.com /2011/03/insidious-devices-an-introduction-to-the-late-american-novel .html.

15. *Code-X: Paper, Ink, Pixel and Screen* (New York: BookRoom Press, 2015), 2.

16. Susan Orlean, "Growing Up in the Library," *New Yorker*, October 5, 2018, https://www.newyorker.com/culture/personal-history /growing-up-in-the-library.

17. Theodore G. Striphas, *The Late Age of Print: Everyday Book Culture from Consumerism to Control* (New York: Columbia University Press, 2009).

18. Rachel Bowlby, *Carried Away: The Invention of Modern Shopping* (New York: Columbia University Press, 2001), 193.

19. Richard Nash, "What Is the Business of Literature?" *Virginia Quarterly Review* 89, no. 2 (2013): 14–27.

20. Striphas, *The Late Age of Print*.

21. Victoria Rideout, *Children, Teens, and Reading: A Common Sense Media Research Brief* (San Francisco: Common Sense Media, 2014), 26.

22. Marylaine Block, *The Thriving Library: Successful Strategies for Challenging Times* (Medford, NJ: Information Today, 2007); Kay Grieves, "The Murray Library Refurbishment," *Library News* 13, March 2014.

23. Sven Birkerts, "Can the 'Literary' Survive Technology?", Literary Hub, April 8, 2016, https://lithub.com/can-the-literary-survive -technology/.

24. Simon Jenkins, "Books Are Back. Only the Technodazzled Thought They'd Go Away," *Guardian*, May 13, 2016, www.theguardian.com /commentisfree/2016/may/13/books-ebook-publishers-paper.

25. Naomi S. Baron, *Words Onscreen: The Fate of Reading in a Digital World* (Oxford, UK: Oxford University Press, 2015).

26. Leah Price, *How to Do Things with Books in Victorian Britain* (Princeton: Princeton University Press, 2012).

27. Amaranth Borsuk, *The Book* (Cambridge, MA: MIT Press, 2018), loc. 2932, Kindle.

28. Customer reviews for Charles Dickens, *David Copperfield* (New York: Penguin Classics, 2016), Amazon, //www.amazon.com/Copperfield -Penguin-Classics-Charles-Dickens/product-reviews/0140439447/ ref=cm_cr_arp_d_viewopt_kywd?filterByKeyword=%22small+print%22&-

search-alias=community-reviews&pageNumber=1#reviews-filter-bar, accessed July 7, 2017.

29. Toni Morrison, *God Help the Child* (New York: Knopf, 2015).

30. Hannah Rosefield, "A Brief History of Oaths and Books," *New Yorker*, June 20, 2014, www.newyorker.com/books/page-turner/a-brief -history-of-oaths-and-books.

31. Marc Fisher, "Donald Trump Doesn't Read Much. Being President Probably Won't Change That," *Washington Post*, July 17, 2016, www .washingtonpost.com/politics/donald-trump-doesnt-read-much-being -president-probably-wouldnt-change-that/2016/07/17/d2ddf2bc-4932 -11e6-90a8-fb84201e0645_story.html?utm_term=.e24317d070f1.

32. "Donald Trump's Bookshelf," *Bookshelf* (blog), January 31, 2017, www.onthebookshelf.co.uk/2017/01/donald-trumps-bookshelf.html ?utm_source=feedburner&utm_medium=feed&utm_campaign=Feed %3A+Bookshelf+%28Bookshelf%29.

33. "Lothair," *Macmillan's* 22 (1870): 153.

34. Frances A. Koestler, *The Unseen Minority: A Social History of Blindness in the United States* (New York: David McKay Co., 1976), 406.

35. Steven G. Kellman, "James Joyce for Ordinary Blokes?", *Chronicle of Higher Education*, September 21, 2009, www.chronicle.com/article /james-joyce-for-ordinary/48427.

36. Flann O'Brien, *The Best of Myles* (Normal, IL: Dalkey Archive Press, 1999), 22.

37. "Books in House Decoration," *New York Times*, April 14, 1878.

38. William H. Sherman, *Used Books: Marking Readers in Renaissance England* (Philadelphia: University of Pennsylvania Press, 2007).

39. Samuel Richardson, *The Paths of Virtue Delineated, or, The History in Miniature of the Celebrated Pamela, Clarissa Harlowe, and Sir Charles Grandison, Familiarised and Adapted to the Capacities of Youth* (London: R. Baldwin, 1756). Held at Houghton Library, Harvard University.

40. Rowan Watson, "Some Non-textual Uses of Books," in *A Companion to the History of the Book*, ed. Simon Eliot and Jonathan Rose (Malden, MA: Blackwell), 485; Thomas Greenwood, *Public Libraries: A History of the Movement and a Manual for the Organization and Management of*

Rate-Supported Libraries (London: Simpkin, Marshall, Hamilton, Kent, & Co., 1890), 494–495.

41. Rollo May, *Man's Search for Himself* (New York: Norton, 1953).

42. H. J. Jackson, *Marginalia: Readers Writing in Books* (New Haven, CT: Yale University Press, 2001).

Chapter 2: The Real Life of Books

1. Victoria Gomelsky, "Watch Brands Looking for New in Era of 'Smart,'" *New York Times*, March 17, 2016, www.nytimes.com/2016/03/17/fashion/watches-baselworld.html.

2. David Sax, "Our Love Affair with Digital Is Over," *New York Times*, November 18, 2017, www.nytimes.com/2017/11/18/opinion/sunday/internet-digital-technology-return-to-analog.html.

3. D. T. Max, "The Last Book," *American Scholar*, May 28, 2001.

4. Henry Stevens, *Recollections of Mr. James Lenox of New York and the Formation of His Library* (London: Henry Stevens & Son, 1887).

5. I owe this point to Isabel Hofmeyr.

6. Simon Eliot, "Some Material Factors in Literary Culture, 2500 BCE–1900 CE," in *Literary Cultures and the Material Book*, ed. Simon Eliot, Andrew Nash, and Ian Willison (London: British Library, 2007), 119.

7. Janet Ing, "The Mainz Indulgences of 1454/5: A Review of Recent Scholarship," *British Library Journal* 9, no. 1 (1983): 14–31.

8. Andrew Pettegree, *The Book in the Renaissance* (New Haven, CT: Yale University Press, 2011), 29.

9. Christopher De Hamel, *The Book: A History of the Bible* (London: Phaidon Press, 2001), 197.

10. Ibid., 206.

11. Paul Duguid, "Material Matters: The Past and Futurology of the Book," in *The Future of the Book*, ed. Geoffrey Nunberg (Berkeley, CA: University of California Press, 1996).

12. Andrew Pettegree, *Brand Luther: 1517, Printing, and the Making of the Reformation* (New York: Penguin Press, 2015), 58.

13. David Mikics, *Slow Reading in a Hurried Age* (Cambridge, MA: Harvard University Press, 2013).

14. James N. Green and Peter Stallybrass, *Benjamin Franklin: Writer and Printer* (New Castle, DE: Oak Knoll Press, 2006).

15. David Reinking, "Valuing Reading, Writing and Books in a Post-Typographic World," in *The Enduring Book: Print Culture in Postwar America*, ed. David Paul Nord, Joan Shelley Rubin, and Michael Schudson (Chapel Hill, NC: University of North Carolina Press, 2009).

16. Aaron Perzanowski and Jason Schultz, *The End of Ownership: Personal Property in the Digital Economy* (Cambridge, MA: MIT Press, 2016).

17. Ibid.

18. Keith Houston, *The Book: A Cover-to-Cover Exploration of the Most Powerful Object of Our Time* (New York: W. W. Norton, 2016), xiv.

19. "New and Cheap Forms of Popular Literature," *Eclectic Review* 22 (1845): 74–84.

20. Honoré de Balzac, *La Cousine Bette* (Paris: Gallimard, 1972), 109.

21. T. Bassett, "Evidence of Reading: The Social Network of the Health Book Club, *Victorian Studies* 59, no. 3 (2016–2017): 429.

22. Ted Striphas, *The Late Age of Print: Everyday Book Culture from Consumerism to Control* (New York: Columbia University Press, 2009), loc. 1445, Kindle.

23. Loren Glass, *Counter-Culture Colophon: Grove Press, the Evergreen Review, and the Incorporation of the Avant-Garde* (Redwood City, CA: Stanford University Press, 2013), 30.

24. Naomi S. Baron, "Redefining Reading: The Impact of Digital Communication Media," *PMLA* 128 (2013): 196; Marcus Wohlsen, "Amazon Wants to Get into the Used E-book Business—or Bury It," *Wired*, February 8, 2013, www.wired.com/2013/02/amazon-used-e-book-patent /; David Streitfeld, "Teacher Knows If You've Done the E-Reading," April 8, 2013, www.nytimes.com/2013/04/09/technology/coursesmart-e -textbooks-track-students-progress-for-teachers.html.

25. Marie Kondo, *The Life Changing Magic of Tidying Up: The Japanese Art of Decluttering and Organizing* (Berkeley, CA: Ten Speed Press, 2014).

26. Myrvold, *Inside the Guru's Gate*.

27. Baron, "Redefining Reading"; Wohlsen, "Amazon Wants."

28. Gregory Cowles, "A Year of Living Better: How to Tap Your Inner Reader," *New York Times*, n.d., https:/nytimes.com/guides/year -of-living-better/how-to-tap-your-inner-reader.

29. Patrick Kingsley, "The Art of Slow Reading," *Guardian*, July 15, 2010, www.guardian.co.uk/books/2010/jul/15/slow-reading.

30. Naomi Tadmor, "'In the Even My Wife Read to Me': Women, Reading, and Household Life in the Eighteenth Century," in *The Practice and Representation of Reading in England*, ed. James Raven, Helen Small, and Naomi Tadmor (Cambridge, UK: Cambridge University Press, 1996), 165.

31. John Plotz, *Semi-Detached: The Aesthetics of Virtual Experience Since Dickens*, (Princeton, NJ: Princeton University Press, 2017).

32. Walter Mischel et al., "Delay of Gratification in Children," *Science* 244, no. 4907 (1989): 933–938.

33. Ann M. Blair, *Too Much to Know: Managing Scholarly Information Before the Modern Age* (New Haven, CT: Yale University Press, 2010).

34. Clifford Lynch, "The Battle to Define the Future of the Book in a Digital World," *First Monday* 6, no. 6 (2001): 9.

35. Ian Rowlands et al., "The Google Generation: The Information Behavior of the Researcher of the Future," *Aslib Proceedings* 60, no. 4 (2008): 290–310.

36. Sven Birkerts, *Changing the Subject: Art and Attention in the Internet Age* (Minneapolis: Graywolf Press, 2015).

37. Erik Kwakkel, "Medieval Kids' Doodles on Birch Bark," on Erik Kwakkel's Tumblr page, posted November 21, 2013, accessed June 24, 2018, http://erikkwakkel.tumblr.com/post/67681966023/medieval -kids-doodles-on-birch-bark-heres.

38. For a forceful critique of classroom "no-device" policies, see Cathy N. Davidson, *The New Education: How to Revolutionize the University to Prepare Students for a World in Flux* (New York: Basic Books, 2017).

39. Baron, *Words Onscreen*.

40. For a survey of studies comparing readers' behavior online and on paper, see Rick Rylance, *Literature and the Public Good: The Literary Agenda* (Oxford, UK: Oxford University Press, 2016).

41. Claudia Fritz et al., "Player Preferences Among New and Old Violins," *Proceedings of the National Academy of Sciences* 109, no. 3 (2012): 760–763.

42. Alan Galey, "The Enkindling Reciter: Ebooks in the Bibliographical Imagination," *Book History* 15, no.1 (2012): 210–247.

43. "FAQ," Google Glass Help, Google, https://support.google.com /glass/answer/3064131, accessed March 27, 2015. See also Katherine Sellgren, "Teenagers 'Checking Mobile Phones in Night,'" BBC, October 26, 2016, www.bbc.com/news/education-37562259.

44. Clay Shirky, "Why Abundance is Good: A Reply to Nick Carr," *Encyclopedia Britannica Blog*, July 17, 2008, http://blogs.britannica.com /2008/07/why-abundance-is-good-a-reply-to-nick-carr/.

45. Michael Harris, *The End of Absence: Reclaiming What We've Lost in a World of Constant Connection* (New York: Current, 2014).

46. Nicholas Carr, "Situational Overload and Ambient Overload," *Rough Type: Nicholas Carr's Blog*, March 7, 2011, www.roughtype.com/?p=1464.

47. John Plotz, "Their Noonday Demons, and Ours," *New York Times*, December 23, 2011, https://www.nytimes.com/2011/12/25/books/review /their-noonday-demons-and-ours.html.

48. Peter Stallybrass, "Books and Scrolls: Navigating the Bible," in *Books and Readers in Early Modern England*, ed. Jennifer Anderson and Elizabeth Sauer (Philadelphia: University of Pennsylvania Press, 2002), 42–79.

49. Nicholas Dames, *The Physiology of the Novel: Reading, Neural Science, and the Form of Victorian Fiction* (Oxford, UK: Oxford University Press, 2007), 18.

50. Mrs. Molesworth, "On the Use and Abuse of Fiction," *Girl's Own Paper*, 13: 452–454.

51. Bobbie Johnson, "Amazon Boss Bezos: Kindle Move Was 'Stupid,'" *Guardian*, July 23, 2009, www.theguardian.com/technology/blog/2009 /jul/24/amazon-drm.

52. Will Self, "The Novel Is Dead (This Time It's for Real)," *Guardian*, May 2, 2014, www.theguardian.com/books/2014/may/02/will-self-novel-dead-literary-fiction.

53. A. M. Paul, "Save the Readers!", *The Brilliant Report: A Monthly Newsletter Bringing You the Latest Intelligence on Learning*, June 9, 2013.

54. Michael Harris, "I Have Forgotten How to Read," *Globe and Mail*, February 9, 2018, www.theglobeandmail.com/opinion/i-have-forgotten-how-toread/article37921379/.

55. Kate Kondayen, "Where Books (and More) Go to Wait," *Harvard Gazette*, September 29, 2014, https://news.harvard.edu/gazette/story/2014/09/where-books-and-more-go-to-wait/.

56. Ben Yakas, "Thanksgiving Day Parade Confetti Made of Confidential Police Docs," Gothamist, November 25, 2012, http://gothamist.com/2012/11/25/thanksgiving_day_parade_confetti_ma.php.

57. "Emma, Le Trefle," YouTube video, 0:38, posted by Le Trefle, March 7, 2013, https://youtube.com/watch?=v-rf7khCkhGk.

Chapter 3: Reading on the Move

1. St. Bergweh, "Jordan Herschel ('s Behavior) Sucks," *St. Bergweh* (blog), June 3, 2015, https://stbergweh.wordpress.com/2015/06/03/jordan-herschel-instagram-influencer-rant/; Kindle (@AmazonKindle), "This summer go camping with your favorite authors," Twitter, June 12, 2015, 12:24 p.m., https://twitter.com/AmazonKindle/status/609441246348771328.

2. On the iconography of the curled-up reading child, see the introduction to Patricia Crain, *Reading Children: Literacy, Property, and the Dilemmas of Childhood in Nineteenth-Century America* (Philadelphia: University of Pennsylvania Press, 2016).

3. Margaret Oliphant, *Miss Marjoribanks* (London: Zodiac Press, 1969).

4. Charlotte Yonge, "Children's Literature: Part III—Class Literature of the Last Thirty Years," *Macmillan's* 20, no. 119 (1869): 454.

5. David Vincent, *The Rise of Mass Literacy: Reading and Writing in Modern Europe* (Cambridge, UK: Polity, 2000); David McKitterick, ed.,

The Cambridge History of the Book in Britain, 1830–1914 (Cambridge, UK: Cambridge University Press, 2009); Stephen Colclough and David Vincent, "Reading," in David McKitterick, ed., *The Cambridge History of the Book in Britain, 1830–1914*.

6. Wendy Griswold, "Glamour and Honor: Going Online and Reading in West African Culture," *Information Technologies and International Development* 3, no. 4: 37–52.

7. Arthur Schopenhauer, *The Art of Literature: A Series of Essays* (London: S. Sonnenschein & Co., 1891), 83.

8. Naomi S. Baron, *Words Onscreen*, loc. 4533, Kindle.

9. Mark Sweney, "'Screen Fatigue' Sees UK Ebook Sales Plunge 17% as Readers Return to Print," *Guardian*, April 27, 2017, www.theguardian.com/books/2017/apr/27/screen-fatigue-sees-uk-ebook-sales-plunge-17-as-readers-return-to-print.

10. "New York Public Library Murals—New York NY," website of the Living New Deal, accessed June 28, 2018, https://livingnewdeal.org/projects/new-york-public-library-murals-new-york-ny/.

11. On Dewey, see Jeffry T. Schnapp and Matthew Battles, *The Library Beyond the Book* (Cambridge, MA: Harvard University Press, 2014), 99–101. On the history of the bookmobile, see William Brown, *Memoir Relative to Itinerating Libraries* (Edinburgh: A. Balfour, 1830) and S. H. Ranck, "Forgotten Traveling Libraries," *Library Journal* 26, no. 5 (1901): 261–265, both discussed in Schnapp and Battles, *The Library Beyond the Book*, 99–101; Kirk Johnson, "Homeless Outreach in Volumes: Books by Bike for 'Outside' People in Oregon," *New York Times*, October 9, 2014, www.nytimes.com/2014/10/10/us/homeless-outreach-in-volumes-books-by-bike-for-outside-people-in-oregon.html.

12. Melvil Dewey, *Field and Future of Traveling Libraries* (Albany: University of the State of New York, 1901), 2.

13. Stewart Brand, "'Keep Designing': How the Information Economy is Being Created and Shaped by the Hacker Ethic," *Whole Earth Review* (May 1985), 49.

14. Walter Benjamin, "Unpacking My Library," in *Illuminations*, ed. Hannah Arendt (New York: Harcourt Brace, 1985).

15. Kenneth Davis, *Two-Bit Culture: The Paperbacking of America* (Boston: Houghton Mifflin, 1984), 56.

16. Quoted in Thomas G. Tanselle, "Reproductions and Scholarship" in *Literature and Artifacts* (Charlottesville, VA: Bibliographical Society of the University of Virginia, 1998), 71.

17. "Kobo Aura H2o: World's First Waterproof eReader Launching in Early 2015, Australian Women Online, November 24, 2014, http:// australianwomenonline.com/kobo-aura-h2o-worlds-first-waterproof -ereader-launching-in-early-2015/; Keither Gessen, "The War of the Words," *Vanity Fair*, December 2014; Jennifer Maloney, "Is 'The Girl on the Train' the New 'Gone Girl'?", *Wall Street Journal*, January 22, 2015, www .wsj.com/articles/is-the-girl-on-the-train-the-new-gone-girl-1421970196.

18. If, as Mark McGurl has argued, "Amazon has undertaken a series of initiatives that suggest a deeper existential commitment to the idea of literature, to getting inside literature, to being literary," one could add that its even deeper commitment is to being bookish. Mark McGurl, "Everything and Less: Fiction in the Age of Amazon," *Modern Language Quarterly* 77, no. 3 (2016): 447–471.

19. Kurt Enoch, "The Paper-Bound Book: Twentieth-Century Publishing Phenomenon," in *The Library Quarterly* 24, no. 3 (1954): 4.

20. Amazon Help, accessed July 1, 2016, www.amazon.com/gp/help /customer/display.html?nodeId=20012748 (page discontinued).

21. "Google Books History," Google Books, accessed July 29, 2015, www.google.com/googlebooks/about/history.html; thanks to Anthony Grafton for the reference. For a magisterial account of the politics of Google Books, see Robert Darnton, *The Case for Books: Past, Present, and Future* (New York: PublicAffairs, 2009).

22. Anthony Grafton, Books and/as New Media presentation, June 2015.

23. Clive Thompson, *Smarter Than You Think: How Technology Is Changing Our Minds for the Better* (New York: Penguin, 2013).

24. This was particularly true before (as Jonathan Grossman explains) the early nineteenth century, when "the network of ruts with 4-foot-deep

holes, called the highways," was replaced by macadamized roads and smoother suspensions. See Jonathan H. Grossman, *The Art of Alibi: English Law Courts and the Novel* (Baltimore: Johns Hopkins University Press, 2002), 17–18.

25. Arthur Lee Humphreys, *The Private Library: What We Do Know, What We Don't Know, What We Ought to Know About Our Books* (London: Strangeways & Sons, 1897), 38.

26. Walter Bagehot, "The First Edinburgh Reviewers," in *Literary Studies*, ed. Richard Holt Hutton (London: Longmans, Green and Co., 1902).

27. Jenny Hartley, "Nineteenth-Century Reading Groups in Britain and the Community of the Text: An Experiment with *Little Dorrit*," in *Reading Communities from Salons to Cyberspace*, ed. DeNel Rehberg Sedo (New York: Palgrave Macmillan, 2011), 53.

28. John Leech, *Punch*, vol. 30 (June 21, 1856), 252.

29. Anne Bowman, *The Common Things of Every-Day Life: A Book of Home Wisdom for Mothers and Daughters* (New York: G. Routledge, 1857), 163.

30. William Godwin, *Memoirs of Mary Wollstonecraft* (New York: Haskell House Publishers Ltd., 1927), 323.

31. *The Gladstone Diaries, Vol. 4: 1848–1854*, ed. M. R. D. Foot and H. C. G. Matthew (Oxford, UK: Oxford University Press, 1974), 375.

32. Rick Rylance, *Literature and the Public Good* (Oxford, UK: Oxford University Press, 2016), 3.

33. Albert Robida, *The Twentieth Century*, ed. Arthur B. Evans, trans. Phillipe Willems (Middletown, CT: Wesleyan University Press, 2004), 4.

34. Harold M. Otness, "Passenger Ship Libraries," *Journal of Library History* 14, no. 1: 492.

35. Matthew Rubery, *The Untold Story of the Talking Book* (Cambridge, MA: Harvard University Press, 2016).

36. Georges Perec, "Reading: A Psycho-Sociological Outline," in *Species of Spaces and Other Pieces*, ed. and trans. John Sturrock (New York: Penguin Books, 1999).

37. E. Annie Proulx, "Books on Top," *New York Times*, May 26, 1994, https://archive.nytimes.com/www.nytimes.com/books/99/05/23/specials /proulx-top.html.

38. Norimitsu Onishi, "Thumbs Race as Japan's Best Sellers Go Cellular," *New York Times*, January 20, 2008, www.nytimes.com/2008/01/20 /world/asia/20japan.html.

39. Charles Dickens, *Dombey and Son* (Oxford, UK: Oxford University Press, 1982), 595.

40. Philip D. Stanhope, "Letter 289," in *Letters Written by Phil. Dormer Stanhope, Earl of Chesterfield, to His Son, Phil. Stanhope, Together with Several Other Pieces* (London: J. Dodsley, 1777), 104. Thanks to Paula McDowell for the reference.

41. See also Philip Waller, *Writers, Readers, and Reputations: Literary Life in Britain, 1870–1918* (Oxford, UK: Oxford University Press, 2018), 48.

42. Leslie Stephen to Anne Isabella Thackeray, 24 April 1870, in *Selected Letters of Leslie Stephen, Vol. 1: 1864–1882*, ed. John W. Bicknell (London: Macmillan, 1996), 80. I found this passage by searching the invaluable Reading Experience Database, www.open.ac.uk/Arts/reading/.

43. Christina Lupton, *Reading and the Making of Time in the Eighteenth Century* (Baltimore: Johns Hopkins University Press, 2018).

44. I'm following here David Henkin's strategy of tracking how often documents such as letters name the day of the week.

45. Sir George Otto Trevelyan, *Life and Letters of Lord Macaulay, Vol. 1* (London: Longmans, Green, and Co., 1876), 60. Available online at https://archive.org/details/lifelettersofor01trevuoft.

46. Hartmut Rosa and Jonathan Trejo-Mathys, *Social Acceleration: A New Theory of Modernity* (New York: Columbia University Press, 2013).

47. Simon Eliot, "Reading by Artificial Light in the Victorian Age," in *Reading and the Victorians*, ed. Matthew Bradley and Juliet John (New York: Ashgate, 2015).

48. Miguel de Cervantes Saavedra, *The History of that Ingenious Gentleman Don Quijote de la Mancha* (London: W. W. Norton & Co., 1996), 1.

49. Jean-Jacques Rousseau, *The Confessions and Correspondence: Including the Letters to Malesherbes* (Lebanon, NH: University Press of New England, 1998), 458.

50. Baron, *Words Onscreen*.

51. Samuel Richardson, in *Selected Letters of Samuel Richardson*, ed. John Carroll (Oxford, UK: Clarendon Press, 1964), 229.

52. Samuel Richardson, *Clarissa, or, The History of a Young Lady: Comprehending the Most Important Concerns of Private Life* (London, 1747), 35.

53. Nikola Tesla, *My Inventions*, first published serially in 1919 in *Electrical Experimenter*, www.teslasautobiography.com/, 17–18.

54. Rob Lucas, "The Critical Net Critic," *New Left Review* 77 (September–October 2012). https://newleftreview.org/II/77/rob-lucas-the-critical-net-critic.

55. Maria Tatar, *Enchanted Hunters: The Power of Stories in Childhood* (New York: W. W. Norton & Co., 2009); Patricia Crain, *Reading Children: Literacy, Property, and the Dilemmas of Childhood in Nineteenth-Century America* (Philadelphia: University of Pennsylvania Press, 2016).

56. "Literature and Mental Health: Reading for Wellbeing," Future Learn, accessed March 29, 2016, www.futurelearn.com/courses/literature.

57. "New Study: 55% of YA Books Bought by Adults," *Publishers Weekly*, September 13, 2012. www.publishersweekly.com/pw/by-topic/childrens/childrens-industry-news/article/53937-new-study-55-of-ya-books-bought-by-adults.html.

58. Natasha Gilmore, "Nielsen Summit Shows the Data Behind the Children's Book Boom," *Publishers Weekly*, September 17, 2015, www.publishersweekly.com/pw/by-topic/childrens/childrens-industry-news/article/68083-nielsen-summit-shows-the-data-behind-the-children-s-book-boom.html.

59. Ruth Graham, "Against YA," *Slate*, June 5, 2014, www.slate.com/articles/arts/books/2014/06/against_ya_adults_should_be_embarrassed_to_read_children_s_books.single.html.

60. Sellgren, "Teenagers 'Checking Mobile Phones.'"

61. Tristan Kirk, "Reading an iPad or Kindle in Bed May Increase Cancer Risk," *Irish Independent*, December 22, 2014, www.independent

.ie/world-news/americas/reading-an-ipad-or-kindle-in-bed-may
-increase-cancer-risk-30854896.html.

62. Anne-Marie Chang, Daniel Aeschbach et. al, "Evening Use of
Light-Emitting eReaders Negatively Affects Sleep, Circadian Timing,
and Next-Morning Alertness," *Proceedings of the National Academy of
Sciences* 112, no. 4 (2015): 1232–1237. The crucial variable appears to be the
wavelength and intensity of light, since the melatonin levels associated
with Kindle use were closer to those associated with printed books than
with a screen emitting short-wavelength blue light. The now-defunct
ebook subscription platform Oyster developed a setting involving less
blue light, in response to its own findings that "reading activity on the
platform peaks between 9 and 10 pm," www.digitalbookworld.com/2015
/oyster-adds-light-sensitive-technology-for-easier-e-reading/ (page discontinued), accessed August 20, 2015.

63. Edward Helmore, "Barnes & Noble: Why It Could Soon Be the
Bookshop's Final Chapter," *Guardian*, May 12, 2018, www.theguardian
.com/books/2018/may/12/barnes-noble-bookstores-retail-amazon.

64. "Devices Used for Reading E-books by Consumers in the
United States as of April 2017," Statista, April 2017, www.statista.com
/statistics/707465/e-book-reading-devices/.

65. Paul Greenberg, "In Search of Lost Screen Time," *New
York Times*, December 31, 2018, www.nytimes.com/2018/12/31/opinion
/smartphones-screen-time.html.

66. Lloyd Shepherd "The Death of Books Has Been Greatly Exaggerated," *Guardian*, August 30, 2011, www.theguardian.com/books/2011
/aug/30/death-books-exaggerated; Katie Arnold-Ratliff, "Soft Target:
Have Reports of the Paperback's Death Been Greatly Exaggerated?",
Slate, June 20, 2013, https://slate.com/technology/2013/06/declining
-sales-of-paperbacks-are-e-readers-killing-the-softcover.html; Christopher Mims, "The Death of the Book Has Been Greatly Exaggerated,"
MIT Technology Review, September 21, 2010, www.technologyreview
.com/s/420881/the-death-of-the-book-has-been-greatly-exaggerated/.

67. Lisa Gitelman, *Paper Knowledge: Toward a Media History of Documents* (Durham, NC: Duke University Press, 2014); Wendy Hui Kyong

Chun, "The Enduring Ephemeral, or the Future is a Memory," *Critical Inquiry* 35, no. 1 (2008): 148–171.

68. "Sunday Reading for the Young," *Public Opinion*, 21, no. 26 (1896): 836.

69. William Morris, *The Ideal Book: Essays and Lectures on the Arts of the Book* (Berkeley, CA: University of California Press, 1982), 65.

70. Frederick G. Kilgour, *The Evolution of the Book* (New York: Oxford University Press, 1998), 3.

71. Jonathan Lazar, "Accessibility," in *Further Reading*, ed. Matthew Rubery and Leah Price (Oxford, UK: Oxford University Press, 2019).

72. Jerome J. McGann, *Black Riders: The Visible Language of Modernism* (Princeton, NJ: Princeton University Press, 1993), 74; see also Aaron Donachuk, "After the Letter: Typographical Distraction and the Surface of Morris's Kelmscott Romances" in *Victorian Studies* 59, no. 2 (2017): 260–287.

73. Tim Wu, "The Tyranny of Convenience," *New York Times*, February 16, 2018, www.nytimes.com/2018/02/16/opinion/sunday/tyranny -convenience.html.

74. John Plotz, *Portable Property: Victorian Culture on the Move* (Princeton, NJ: Princeton University Press, 2008), 158; Elizabeth Carolyn Miller, *Slow Print: Literary Radicalism and Late Victorian Print Culture* (Stanford, CA: Stanford University Press, 2013).

Interleaf: Please Lay Flat

1. Rayomand Engineer, "Kids Weighed Down by School Bags? Here's What the Future of Education Can Look Like," The Better India, December 14, 2017, www.thebetterindia.com/124442/heavy-school-bags -children-health-problems-solution/. Thanks to Priyasha Mukhopadh-yay for passing this along.

2. See also Matthew Brown, "Book Reviews: *Unpacking My Library: Writers and Their Books*," *Openings: Studies in Book Art*, no. 1 (2012): 80–83.

3. Craig Mod, "A Simpler Page," *A List Apart*, January 11, 2011, http: //alistapart.com/article/a-simpler-page.

4. Lucy Helen Muriel Soulsby, *Stray Thoughts on Reading* (London: Longmans, Green, and Co., 1898), 6.

5. E. R. Hudders, *Indexing and Filing: A Manual of Standard Practice* (New York: Ronald Press, 1919), 59. Thanks to Craig Robertson for the reference.

6. Vladimir Nabokov interview with *Playboy*, January 1964, transcribed at http://kulichki.com/moshkow/NABOKOW/Intero3.txt.

7. Peter Stallybrass, "Books and Scrolls: Navigating the Bible," in *Books and Readers in Early Modern England*, ed. Jennifer Andersen and Elizabeth Sauer (Philadelphia: University of Pennsylvania Press, 2002), 42–79.

8. Octave Uzanne, "The End of Books," *Scribner's*, July–December 1894; Matthew Rubery, *The Untold Story of the Talking Book* (Cambridge, MA: Harvard University Press, 2016), 46–54.

Chapter 4: Prescribed Reading

1. Neil Frude, *Book Prescription Wales 2011—A Strategy for Enhancing Treatment Choice for Mental Health: Prescriber Information Booklet*, Wales National Health Service, 2011, www.wales.nhs.uk/sitesplus/documents /829/BPW%20Prescriber%20Information%20booklet%20.pdf.

2. Ibid.

3. Mark Brown, "GPs to Prescribe Self-Help Books for Mental Health Problems," *Guardian*, January 31, 2013, www.theguardian.com /society/2013/jan/31/gps-prescribe-self-help-books.

4. "Reading Well Books on Prescription Reaches over 100,000 People in First Three Months," The Reading Agency, n. d., https://reading agency.org.uk/adults/news/reading-well-books-on-prescription -reaches-over-100000-people-in-first-three-months.html. A total of 75,654 copies of *Fifty Shades of Grey* were borrowed from UK libraries in 2012–2013: "Which Were the Most Borrowed Library Books in 2012– 2013?," *Guardian*, February 14, 2014, www.theguardian.com/news/data blog/2014/feb/14/most-borrowed-library-books-2012-13. The figure is from the Public Lending Right's "100 Most Borrowed Books 2012/2013

UK," www.bl.uk/britishlibrary/~/media/bl/global/services/plr/pdfs/most borrowedtitles2012-13/uk.pdf.

5. Alice Munro, *Too Much Happiness* (London: Chatto & Windus, 2009), 124 and 48.

6. Pamela Duncan and Nicola Davis, "Four Million People in England Are Long-Term Users of Antidepressants," *Guardian*, August 10, 2018, www.theguardian.com/society/2018/aug/10/four-million-people-in-england-are-long-term-users-of-antidepressants; National Center for Health Statistics, "Antidepressant Use Among Persons Aged 12 and Over: United States, 2011–2014," NCHS Data Brief No. 283, August 2017, Centers for Disease Control and Prevention, www.cdc.gov/nchs/products/databriefs/db283.htm.

7. Catrin Lewis, Jennifer Pearce, and Jonathan I. Bisson, "Efficacy, Cost-Effectiveness and Acceptability of Self-Help Interventions for Anxiety Disorders: Systematic Review." *British Journal of Psychiatry* 200, no. 1 (2012): 15–21.

8. "What is new in this treatment modality is not the content, because bibliotherapy usually uses a cognitive-behavioral approach. Only the form in which it is presented is new," according to Pim Cuijpers, "Bibliotherapy in Unipolar Depression: A Meta-Analysis," *Journal of Behavior Therapy and Experimental Psychiatry* 28, no. 2 (1997): 139–147.

9. Frude, *Book Prescription Wales 2011*.

10. NICE Technology Appraisal, "Computerised Cognitive Behavior Therapy for Depression and Anxiety," in *Review of Technology Appraisal*, February 22, 2006; Pim Cuijpers and Josien Schuurmans, "Self-Help Interventions for Anxiety Disorders: An Overview," *Current Psychiatry Reports* 9, no. 4 (2007): 284–290; University of Zurich, "Psychotherapy via Internet as Good as If Not Better Than Face-to-Face Consultations," Science Daily, July 30, 2013, www.sciencedaily.com/releases/2013/07/130730091255.htm.

11. Frude, *Book Prescription Wales 2011*.

12. A PLOS One study acknowledges "the exclusion of people with low energy, concentration difficulty and tiredness. The rationale was to focus on people who could use the materials—but this excluded a small

number of people with some 'core' symptoms of depression." See Christopher Williams et al., "Guided Self-Help Cognitive Behavioural Therapy for Depression in Primary Care: A Randomised Controlled Trial," PLOS One, January 11, 2013, doi: 10.1371/journal.pone.0052735.

13. Susannah Fox, "The Social Life of Health information," Pew Research Center, January 15, 2014, www.pewresearch.org/fact-tank/2014/01/15/the-social-life-of-health-information/.

14. Prem Ramaswami, "A Remedy for Your Health-Related Questions: Health Info in the Knowledge Graph," *The Keyword* (blog), Google, February 10, 2015, https://blog.google/products/search/health-info-knowledge-graph/.

15. Mary Giliberty, "Learning More About Clinical Depression with the PHQ-9 Questionnaire," *The Keyword* (blog), Google, August 23, 2017, www.blog.google/products/search/learning-more-about-clinical-depression-phq-9-questionnaire/.

16. Samuel Smiles, *Self-Help, with Illustrations of Character, Conduct, and Perseverance* (Chicago: Belford, Clarke, and Co., 1884).

17. Ibid.

18. William Kite, "Fiction in Public Libraries," *American Library Journal* 1, no. 8 (1877): 278.

19. Francis X. Clines, "Indie Bookstores Are Back, with a Passion," *New York Times*, February 12, 2016, www.nytimes.com/2016/02/13/opinion/indie-bookstores-are-back-with-a-passion.html.

20. John Durham Peters, *The Marvelous Clouds: Toward a Philosophy of Elemental Media* (Chicago: University of Chicago Press, 2015), 186.

21. James Henry Clark, *Sight and Hearing: How Preserved, and How Lost* (New York: C. Scribner, 1859).

22. Isaac Ray, *Mental Hygiene*, in *American Journal of the Medical Sciences* 47 (1864).

23. Ibid., 56.

24. Ibid., 243 and 56.

25. Ibid., 376.

26. American Female Guardian Society, "Education of Women," *Advocate and Family Guardian* 30, no. 17 (1864): 199.

27. Anonymous, "Novels as Sedatives," *Spectator* 73 (1894): 108.

28. Rich McManus, "Professor Traces Nation's 'Drinking Age Debates,'" *NIH Record* 63, no. 19 (2011), https://nihrecord.nih.gov/newsletters /2011/09_16_2011/story1.htm.

29. Quoted in Michael Denning, *Mechanic Accents; Dime Novels and Working-Class Culture in America* (London: Verso, 1998).

30. Anonymous, "Reading Dissipation," *Journal of Education*, April 4, 1901.

31. Angelo Patri, "Too Much Reading is Harmful," *St. Petersburg Times*, June 29, 1938.

32. Samuel McChord Crothers, "A Literary Clinic," *Atlantic Monthly*, September 1916.

33. Robert Haven Schauffler, *The Poetry Cure; A Pocket Medicine Chest of Verse* (New York: Dodd, Mead and Co., 1925), xxxv.

34. Ibid, xxxi.

35. Sadie Delaney, "The Place of Bibliotherapy in a Hospital," *Library Journal* 63 (April 15, 1938): 305.

36. D. Pehrsson and P. S. McMillen, "A Bibliotherapy Evaluation Tool: Grounding Counselors in the Therapeutic Use of Literature." *The Arts in Psychotherapy* 32, no. 1 (2005): 47–59.

37. Quoted in the film *James Baldwin: The Price of the Ticket*, directed by Karen Thorsen (1989).

38. John Duffy, Jo Haslam, Lesley Holl, and Julie Walker, "Bibliotherapy Toolkit," March 2010.

39. Gina McOuat, "The Librarian as Rehabilitator," *Bibliothecha Medica Canadiana* 7, no. 3 (1985): 4.

40. Meredith Martin, *The Rise and Fall of Meter: Poetry and English National Culture, 1860–1930* (Princeton, NJ: Princeton University Press, 2012).

41. Brian A. Primack et al., "Using Ecological Momentary Assessment to Determine Media Use by Individuals with and Without Major Depressive Disorder," *JAMA* 165, no. 4 (2011): 360–365.

42. "Reading Well Evidence Base," The Reading Agency, http://readingagency.org.uk/adults/impact/research/reading-well-books-on-prescription-scheme-evidence-base.html. The Reading Agency explained in 2012 that "our Mood-boosting Books promotion is aimed at adults, particularly those who *might* have experienced mild to moderate mental-health conditions linked to stress, anxiety and depression" (emphasis mine). See also "Mood-boosting Books 2012," Reading Groups for Everyone, http://readinggroups.org/news/mood-boosting-books-2012.html.

43. Avni Bavishi, Martin D. Slade, and Becca R. Levy, "A Chapter a Day: Association of Book Reading with Longevity," *Social Science and Medicine* 164 (2016): 44–48.

44. Associated Press, "NYC Hospitals to Offer Veggie 'Prescriptions,'" Fox News, July 25, 2013, www.foxnews.com/health/2013/07/25/nyc-hospitals-to-offer-veggie-prescriptions.html#ixzz2aI9IcxmP.

45. On the rise of therapeutic culture, see Timothy Aubry and Trysh Travis, eds., *Rethinking Therapeutic Culture* (Chicago: University of Chicago Press, 2015).

46. Sarah Sloat, "'Book Doctors' Say What You Need Is a Good Read," *Wall Street Journal*, December 18, 2016, www.wsj.com/articles/book-doctors-say-what-you-need-is-a-good-read-1482091512.

47. http://biblioconcierge.com/, accessed February 10, 2014.

48. Susan Elderkin and Ella Berthoud, *The Novel Cure: An A–Z of Literary Remedies* (Edinburgh: Canongate Books, 2013), 266.

49. Birkerts, *Changing the Subject*.

50. Beth Blum, "The Self-Help Hermeneutic: Its Global History and Literary Future," *PMLA* 133, no. 5 (2018): 1099–1117.

51. Compare Boris Kachka's observation that "today, every section of the store (or web page) overflows with instructions, anecdotes, and homilies. History books teach us how to lead, neuroscience how to use our amygdalas, and memoirs how to eat, pray, and love," in "The Power of Positive Publishing: How Self-Help Ate America," *New York*, January 6, 2013, http://nymag.com/health/self-help/2013/self-help-book-publishing/.

52. Shirky, "Why Abundance is Good."

53. Edward L. Deci, *Intrinsic Motivation* (New York: Plenum Press, 1975).

Chapter 5: Bound by Books

1. Sara Nelson, *So Many Books, So Little Time: A Year of Passionate Reading* (New York: Berkley, 2003); Seth Lerer, "Epilogue: Falling Asleep over the History of the Book," *PMLA* 121, no. 1, (2006): 229–234; Mikita Brottman, *The Solitary Vice: Against Reading* (Berkeley: Counterpoint, 2008); Rick Gekoski, *Outside of a Dog: A Bibliomemoir* (London: Constable, 2009).

2. Yusuf Kassam, "Who Benefits from Illiteracy? Literacy and Empowerment," in *The Challenge of Illiteracy: From Reflection to Action*, ed. Zaghloul Morsy (New York: Garland, 1994), 33.

3. Carolyn Miller et al., "Parents, Children, Libraries, and Reading," Pew Research Center, May 1, 2013, www.pewinternet.org/2013/05/01 /parents-children-libraries-and-reading/.

4. David Vincent, *Literacy and Popular Culture: England 1750–1914* (Cambridge, UK: Cambridge University Press, 1989), 259.

5. Michèle Petit, *L'art de lire, ou, Comment résister à l'adversité* (Paris: Belin, 2008), 114.

6. Thomas Greenwood, *Public Libraries: A History of the Movement and a Manual for the Organization and Management of Rate-Supported Libraries* (London: Simpkin Marshall, 1890).

7. Marie Corelli, *Free Opinions Freely Expressed on Certain Phases of Modern Social Life and Conduct* (London: Archibald Constable, 1905), 9.

8. Wayne A. Wiegand, *Part of Our Lives: A People's History of the American Public Library* (Oxford, UK: Oxford University Press, 2015), 239.

9. Sarah Dudek, "Refugees Welcome: Library Membership Cards for Refugees in Berlin—First Numbers After Four Months," *IFLA Public Libraries Section Blog*, February 7, 2016, https://blogs.ifla.org/public -libraries/2016/02/07/refugees-welcome-library-membership-cards -for-refugees-in-berlin-first-numbers-after-four-months/. For a similar

program in Cologne, see Ross Davies, "Cologne Library Opens Its Doors to Refugees: 'You Fill This Room with Life'", *Guardian*, February 21, 2017, www.theguardian.com/cities/2017/feb/21/cologne-library-opens-doors -refugees-you-fill-room-with-life.

10. Deborah Brandt, *Literacy and Learning: Reflections on Writing, Reading, and Society* (San Francisco: Jossey-Bass, 2009), 19.

11. Andrew Piper, *Book Was There: Reading in Electronic Times* (Chicago: University of Chicago Press, 2012), 84.

12. Lady Bradshaigh to Samuel Richardson, 16 December 1749, in *Correspondence of Samuel Richardson, Author of Pamela, Clarissa, and Sir Charles Grandison: Selected from the Original Manuscripts*, ed. Anna Laetitia Barbauld (London: Richard Phillips, 1804), 305.

13. Interview with Jane Davis, London, September 11, 2013.

14. Howley, "In the Ancient World," *Further Reading*, forthcoming.

15. On modern devotional reading, see Paul J. Griffiths, *Religious Reading: The Place of Reading in the Practice of Religion* (New York: Oxford University Press, 1999). On print culture in Alcoholics Anonymous, see Trysh Travis, *The Language of the Heart: A Cultural History of the Recovery Movement from Alcoholics Anonymous to Oprah Winfrey* (Chapel Hill, NC: University of North Carolina Press, 2009), 11–14, 107–108.

16. Maggie Downs, "How the Silent Book Club Gave Back My Reading Life," Literary Hub, August 16, 2017, https://lithub.com/how -the-silent-book-club-gave-me-back-my-reading-life/.

17. Elizabeth Long, *Book Clubs: Women and the Uses of Reading in Everyday Life* (Chicago: University of Chicago Press, 2003), 165.

18. Philip Oltermann, "Hannibal Lecter Saved My Life," *Guardian*, March 31, 2007, www.theguardian.com/books/2007/mar/31/features reviews.guardianreview1.

19. R. K. Dent, "Introduction to a Discussion on the Blacking Out of Sporting News in Free Libraries," *Library* 6, no. 1 (1894): 127–129.

20. Arthur E. Bostwick, *The Library and Society: Reprints of Papers and Addresses* (New York: Wilson, 1920).

21. Julie Hersberger, "The Homeless and Information Needs and Services," *Reference and User Services Quarterly* 44, no. 3 (2005): 202.

22. Amir Efrati, "Google's Brin Gives Los Altos a Lift," *Wall Street Journal*, August 29, 2012, www.wsj.com/articles/SB10000872396390444506004577615261807454988; Judith Rosen, "Judy Blume, Bookseller," *Publishers Weekly*, April 14, 2016, www.publishersweekly.com/pw/by-topic/childrens/childrens-authors/article/69960-judy-blume-bookseller.html.

23. "About Us," Concord Free Press, www.concordfreepress.com.

24. Stona Fitch, "Free Books," *Publishers Weekly*, March 8, 2010, www.publishersweekly.com/pw/by-topic/columns-and-blogs/soapbox/article/42343-soapbox-free-books.html. See also Piper, *Book Was There*, 83.

25. Simone Murray, *The Digital Literary Sphere: Reading, Writing and Selling Books in the Internet Era* (Baltimore: Johns Hopkins University Press, 2018).

26. Marie Lebert, *Project Gutenberg (1971–2008)*, Project Gutenberg, www.gutenberg.org/ebooks/27045.

27. Interview with Davis.

28. Michael Warner, "Uncritical Reading," in *Polemic: Critical or Uncritical*, ed. Jane Gallop (New York: Routledge, 2004); Merve Emre, *Paraliterary: The Making of Bad Readers in Postwar America* (Chicago: University of Chicago Press, 2017).

End Papers

1. "Readmember," HackDash, https://hackdash.org/projects/56929c4d62b2cc5d050af727.

2. https://github.com/mailbackwards/litcity, accessed September 1, 2018.

3. Interview in *New York Dramatic Mirror* (July 1913), quoted in "Books Will Soon Be Obsolete in the Schools," Quote Investigator, February 15, 2012, https://quoteinvestigator.com/2012/02/15/books-obsolete/.

4. Arundell James Kennedy Esdaile, *Autolycus' Pack, and Other Light Wares: Being Essays, Addresses and Verses* (London: Grafton & Co., 1940), 182; Jane Howard, "Close-Up," *Life*, February 25, 1966: 92; thanks to Geoff Nunberg for this point.

5. Balmer, R. "Whispering Machines," *Nineteenth Century* 17 (1885): 496–499, 497.

6. Stanislaw Lem, *Return from the Stars* (New York: Harvest, 1961), 79.

7. Henry T. Coutts, *Library Jokes and Jottings: A Collection of Stories Partly Wise but Mostly Otherwise* (London: Grafton & Co., 1914), 149.

8. Esdaile, *Autolycus' Pack*, 140.

9. Ray Bradbury, "Pillar of Fire," in *Match to Flame: The Fictional Paths to Fahrenheit 451*, ed. Donn Albright and Jon R. Eller, (Colorado Springs, CO: Gauntlet Press, 2006), 113.

INDEX

JON CHASE

LEAH PRICE has taught English at Cambridge University, Harvard University, and Rutgers University, where from fall 2019 onward she will be founding director of the Rutgers Book Initiative. She is the author of *The Anthology and the Rise of the Novel* and *How to Do Things with Books in Victorian Britain* and the editor of *Unpacking My Library: Writers and Their Books.*